FIELD RECORDINGS FROM THE INSIDE

ALSO BY JOE BONOMO

FIELD RECORDINGS FROM THE INSIDE

JOE BONOMO

Essays

SOFT SKULL PRESS
BERKELEY

Library of Congress Cataloging-in-Publication Data

Names: Bonomo, Joe, 1966- author.
Title: Field recordings from the inside : essays / Joe Bonomo.
Description: Berkeley, CA : Soft Skull Press, [2017] | Includes bibliographical references.
Identifiers: LCCN 2016040601 | ISBN 9781593766627
Subjects: LCSH: Popular music--History and criticism.
Classification: LCC ML3470 .B69 2017 | DDC 781.6409--dc23
LC record available at https://lccn.loc.gov/2016040601

Cover design by Faceout Studio
Interior design by Megan Jones Design

ISBN 978-1-59376-662-7

Soft Skull Press
An Imprint of Counterpoint
2560 Ninth Street, Suite 318
Berkeley, CA 94710
www.softskull.com

Printed in the United States of America
Distributed by Publishers Group West

10 9 8 7 6 5 4 3 2 1

For Amy

Every human being is an archaeological site.

—LUC SANTE

ORIGIN STORIES

ORN OF A mathematician and a nurse into the lime-green cradle of the suburbs, fifth of six kids, Patty Hearst on *TIME* and the fall of Saigon, windows onto a troubling landscape, early lessons in magic at the Wheaton Rec Center and bike rides into and out of woods that promised solitude and necking couples—but I really want to steal the origin story of my younger brother, who at age one was holding himself up on the stereo cabinet in the living room watching a record go around—it was Sinatra or Wes Montgomery or Paul Revere & the Raiders—when he turned and for the first time in his life walked upright, beaming, a song behind him.

SCHOOL STARTED AGAIN in the fall, my tan faded, I trudged into Saint Andrew the Apostle with scissors, Elmer's glue, a pencil case, and brand-new textbooks with pages that were blurry yet vivid to the touch. I looked down at my feet, they were there and they weren't; in my head, or from a passing car, 10cc's "The Things We Do for Love" was playing.

AT HOME, AN open notebook on a desk, James Dean on the wall, siblings in the hall, half-there, half-invisible, I'd look out my bedroom window at dusk and see half-world, half-me, before I learned the term "rack focus," the world, back to me, the world, back to me, the world, back to me, below, kids walked to homes I'd never see, though I'd imagine them. In my head, or from a passing car, Cheap Trick's "Dream Police" was playing.

THE 45 TWELVE-PACK from Korvettes spun in rotation on the family stereo and the Sweet's "Little Willy" became as real as my real friends, until the day my older brother sat on the record on the living room couch, cracking the single for good, and then I learned the sadness of broken records—F. Scott Fitzgerald compared his nervous breakdown to a cracked dinner plate; I'll call adolescent sadness a cracked 45, irreparable, for-good gone, and the analog era of snapped tape and busted 8-tracks and torn album covers crept forward, and all of the kitchen Scotch tape in all of Wheaton could not splice together the Dart Drug cassettes lost to mean feet or indifference or random tosses down the basement steps.

IN THE BASEMENT Era all you needed was a steady hand, a screwdriver, some Scotch tape, and the nerve to believe that a cassette tape could be broken into, and if you were lucky not to fatally crack the plastic case and get in, the world inside was promising, somehow comforting in its *thereness*, its motocross of tape and spindles over which you hover in a kind of preteen omniscience, your fingers impossibly large, trembling now to find and lift one end of the snapped tape and with a sliver of Scotch tape marry it back to the other end, all the while feeling, because you'd watched *The Wizard of Oz* again with the family last night, that you've pulled aside the curtain, magic and private, the cassette tape vanishing and emerging from a dark you've now flooded with basement fluorescent light, humming, nervous as you reattach the plastic housing, hoping against hope that when you press play the homespun little-boy mend won't catch on the tape heads and split again, not aware even in your deepest imagination that one day tape will recede from the basements and bedrooms and rec rooms and from beneath tires on the driveway and the streets out front, that one day the dark that you've imagined inside your Certron C90, the dark you cracked as puberty loomed and all sorts of unsolvable mysteries upstairs threatened, the dark entered with the suburban toolkit of tape-and-wish would merge with an anti-language spoken in ones and zeros, the dark that once seemed impenetrable would come to be seen as less a mystery to ponder than a digital *nothingthere* to never quite understand, a dark that stymies boys when they have the urge to fix things. *Keep out.*

A SCRATCH ON a 45 or an album was the uninvited bully, the mean kid who shows up at your party, a little gouge you'd see with a sinking stomach as you held the album up to the light to reveal the chip, the dent, the cut. We'd try to shoo away the skip by placing a penny on the tone arm or, when that didn't work and we were feeling bold or desperate enough, by pressing down ever so lightly on the cartridge as the skip approached— right after the chorus or right when the solo starts or during the first line of the bridge, the interruption you'd come to know as a wound that never healed right—my finger shaking slightly, and I'm hoping for just the right touch, just the right balance between pressure and lift so when that skip comes the needle will move right through, unafraid, and the next time we play the album the needle will play right through him again and eventually he'll get the message.

IF I DIDN'T succeed, if I lost my Zen-like poise there in the basement or if the gouge was just too deep, no magic touch could finesse that scratch out of the room; he was there for good, the unwanted stepsibling, the weird cousin who came for the summer but stayed, blinking at a past of melancholy at which you could only guess—there for good, to trip the song into permanent disability. Yes, a scratch was like that, a figure out of bad dreams who showed up one day and stayed. No amount of gentle laying-on-of-hands or Windex or dusting or praying would ever get rid of him, and the world would go out of focus and back into clarity and something would change for good, though you couldn't name exactly what.

JOE O. WAS in the rec room, struggling to play the simple opening chords of Foreigner's "Cold as Ice" on the piano, and I was upstairs in my bedroom—upset about something, red-faced, strangely sequestered that day from the kid I was playing with, the same Joe who lived with nearly a dozen siblings stacked two to a bed in a tiny red box of a house on Nairn, the boy I went to kindergarten with and who got in trouble with me when we slid on our knees, side-grins at each other, that language, the boy who went to Saint Andrew with me, growing into the man he'd become, who was more athletic, the day at recess when the bell rang as the football he threw at the tail end of a play precisely designed zipped on a line into my ribs, stinging terribly, the same boy who in an act of betrayal to my childish leanings went to a different high school where he wasn't big enough to play football so he volunteered to run the first-down markers during the game against Good Counsel, where I watched from the bleachers feigning disinterest as he marched up and down the field, a small adult now, barking orders, speaking in a foreign language to kids I didn't know— alone, trying to make sense of the promises made by a pop song badly played by a friend downstairs who was already, although I didn't know it then, leaving.

I THOUGHT THAT Terry Jacks was dying, that "Seasons in the Sun," which played endlessly on AM radio that year, was his goodbye letter to the world, that as he sang he knew that he was dying, that his body was shutting down, the melody and the words a gentle but tragic farewell to his family and his friends, their mammoth grief now shared with millions, none of this really explainable to me, neither by my older brothers nor by myself, how a song could exist on the radio that was so sad, so utterly sad, not sad in the way "The Night the Lights Went Out in Georgia" or "Daniel" was sad, or in the way that the theme from *Love Story* was sad, the simple melody of which was everywhere for a while then, too, but throat-tightening sad, a song that as it played made me desperate to turn to my brothers and sister in the rec room or in the car and ask *Why?*, why is this happening, why is Casey Kasem playing this man's death song, how can something so sad be so public, and why are your friends laughing, none of these ideas really available to me at the time but in the language that my cold chest spoke when the song came on WPGC and I again pictured Terry Jacks on his deathbed in a hospital, his weeping family around him, or— is he dead already? is the song I'm listening to a melody and a clenched apology for mortality issuing from the grave? and either way it was a desolate season for me, the start of something ineffable, the unhappy, unwanted blend of a singsong melody and grief, popular radio on a sunny Saturday afternoon and half-thoughts of death and dying, all of it a blur of presentiment and incomprehension, and when the song disappeared, as all Top 40 songs do, I thought that Terry Jacks, whoever he was, wherever he was, went with it too, gone forever but for this wrenching goodbye trailing him, until years later when I learned that nah, Jacks is alive, somewhere up in Canada, he'd never died or been ill when he released the song, urban legend, it was a cover of some old French song anyway, and get this, the B-side of the single, you're not gonna believe it, was called "Put the Bone In"!—all the adolescent irony I'd need to erase, for a while, the season of sadness.

FIELD RECORDINGS
FROM THE INSIDE

*M*Y YOUNGER BROTHER had developed a phobia of listening to records played at the wrong speeds. We'd be listening to a 45 or an LP, and if I moved the RPM knob one way or the other and the song lurched into nasal, pinched hysteria or growled down to a menacing dirge, Paul would cover his ears, his eyes flashing. Sometimes he'd dash from the room; sometimes he'd cry. I can't claim largesse these many decades later, manfully acknowledging that I soothed my younger brother in his distress—once in a while I'd torture him, quickly switching a record to the wrong speed to see his (predictable) reaction. Older-Sibling Job Description, maybe, but an unkind responsibility not without its trails of remorse. Inside of me: that a record could be insidious, that music has an interior darkness I didn't know about. Look what it can do.

IN THE SPRING and summer of 1975, "I'm Not in Love" by 10cc was in regular rotation in the Top 40, reigning for two weeks at number one on the U.K. charts and peaking at num-ber two on *Billboard*. Composed by Eric Stewart and Graham Gouldman, the song is famous for its haunting tones and oth-erworldly choral effect, studio-created by massing more than 250 vocal harmonies, a mammoth, labor-intensive undertak-ing in the era before digital sampling. Band members Stewart, Gouldman, Kevin Godley, and Lol Creme each sang a single note in unison that was then mixed, dubbed, and re-dubbed across sixteen tracks, looped, then played in a heartbreaking descending-then-ascending melody via keyboards and faders. An airy construction, the song begins in medias res, the instru-mentation spare throughout: a Fender organ in the left chan-nel mutters softly, a bass drum thumps quietly in the center, a strummed acoustic guitar whispers in the right. The effect might be the closest a pop song has ever gotten to reproducing a dream, the loose ends of experience beyond language. "I'm Not in Love" is less a tune than a field recording from the inside of your body, your heart chambers' *vérité*.

There's tension in the deceptively sweetly-sung lyric: self-absorbed, defensive sentiments threaten to pop the bubble of that ethereality, casual but controlling barbs insisting that the singer's detached, too uncaring to be in love, that your photo's only covering a stain on the wall, you'll wait a long time for me and if I call you don't make a fuss and don't tell your friends. Is that 10cc's game? Subverting the dream with cool indifference? Nothing so ghostly gorgeous can last long when, beneath it all, there's an insecure man threatening to destroy it. (When R.E.M. composed their striking quasi-homage to "I'm Not in Love"— "Star Me Kitten" on 1992's *Automatic for the People*—they morphed these tensions into post-punk lewdness, Michael Stipe later revealing that the "star me" in the title was the equivalent to an asterisk demurely blotting out the phrase "fuck me.")

I knew what "I'm Not in Love" was about, when I couldn't possibly have known. More: I understood the tensions and psychologies among the callousness of the words, the icy distance in the vocals, the dreaminess of the melody and arrangement— before I could understand such grown-up things. Is it possible for an epiphany to be scored? What is knowledge in a pop song? William Hazlitt: "You know more of a road by having traveled it than by all the conjectures and descriptions in the world." I'm not so sure. At age nine or so, I hadn't yet journeyed down the roads of infatuation and heartbreak when I first heard "I'm Not in Love," far from it; I hadn't even imagined them sentimentally from my bedroom window. I was puzzling over smiling teases from girls on the playground, my older sister's crushes, and countenances that hinted at a language beyond the one I spoke, stumbling words that clearly failed as choral "ahhhs" from the radio transcended.

AROUND THE TIME that "I'm Not in Love" was on the radio entrancing and frightening me, my parents purchased a double album, *The Beatles 1962–1970*. But this was an album not by the Beatles, sadly, but by Kings Road, and not on the cheery bright-green Apple label but on a label called Pickwick. What I didn't know then: Pickwick was a notorious budget label borne in the 1950s from the ashes of a children's music label. By the late 1960s/early 1970s, president and owner Cy Leslie was raking it in from issuing compilations mimicking the top hits of the year by bands like Kings Road (other outfits were Mirror Image and Top of the Pops).

These albums confound me now. Tacitly of the K-Tel/Ronco era, they ended up on the floors of basements and bedrooms, spun on the family stereo or in private by disenchanted kids who'd been stoked while unwrapping the album to have a collection of Top 40 hits. What did we kids know about licensing? About "cut-rate?" About the bottom line? Moments after the needle drops on the first song—the latest smash by Carly Simon or Bread or Johnny Nash—you know that something's not right. The timbre of the voice, the flatness of the playing, the squashed production conspire within moments to say to you, *You've been ripped off*. Welcome to another adolescent disappointment. Whatever satisfactions that barely dressed, smiling hippie girl on the brightly colored front jacket provided, they were short-lived. *This sucks*, I'd say to myself, watching the turntable spin.

Around this time, a group of kids at Saint Andrew the Apostle School during recess linked their hands and danced in a circle crying, "The witch is dead, the witch is dead!" They were mocking the memory of an unpopular substitute teacher to whom we'd been ghastly, and who'd moved to Florida and, we heard, died there. My friends' glee made me nauseated and gloomy, though I likely joined the chanting. I felt a similar nameless misery listening to Kings Road: intuiting the sadness of vulnerable grown-ups, a weakness that all kids witness eventually in the movement between ignorance and knowledge. Kings Road was a virtual band, comprised of session musicians cobbled together to knock off a stack of songs-per-session, on time, under budget. As the musicians bluffed their way through "Please Please Me," "I Want to Hold Your Hand," "Michelle," "Hey Jude" (which they dutifully, dreadfully aped for nearly six minutes), "The Long and Winding Road," and solo tracks like "Junk," "My Sweet Lord," and, improbably, the emotionally raw "Mother," my brothers and I guffawed, breaking up at the lame singing and playing, so obviously "*not* the Beatles!" An earnest attempt at gaming consumers turned into a half-serious aural joke that soon morphed into something beyond funny, into surreal wretchedness. Listening to Kings Road, I felt unnamed pity for the musicians even as I was making fun of them.

In particular I remember their soft rendition of "Revolution," the amateur screeching, the compressed, white fury of Lennon's Epiphone Casino guitar reduced to something that sounded like the anemic buzz of a malfunctioning electric razor. The ferocious drumming? Overturned oatmeal canisters struck with pencils. (And out of time, at that.) The performances were hilariously inept, and now I wonder at the premise of such budget LPs: to whom were they marketed? Certainly Pickwick cared more about moving units than disenchanting kids, but the executives in their boardroom didn't consider the effects such albums would have on the gullible. What was meant to sound like earnest tribute and celebration fell on my ears as desperate and embarrassing. This much I understood as the album spun around and around: Kings Road were the weary substitute teachers of pop music.

"INTELLECT CONFUSES INTUITION," says Piet Mondrian. On long afternoons when I wasn't down in the rec room puzzling over Kings Road, I was listening to *Elvis: As Recorded at Madison Square Garden*. At the time I wasn't a big Elvis fan— no one in my family was, really; we imitated him (we had a compilation album of Elvis sound-alikes, too). I wouldn't come to appreciate him for many years. I was a kid, and I thought that his bright-white rhinestone-studded bell-bottom jumpsuit on the album jacket was the coolest thing in the world, his legs-splayed, finger-snapping pose a kind of foreign language, and I liked the up-tempo songs. (A recording of a performance from June of 1972, the album was, in Colonel Tom Parker's "Taking Care of Business" style, on sale in record and department stores little more than a week after the concert. I have the album still, the cover held together with Scotch tape.)

I especially loved the way the record opened. Ascending from the vinyl's clicks and pops: the dramatic notes of Richard

Strauss's tone poem "Also Sprach Zarathustra," known popu-
larly as the theme from *2001: A Space Odyssey*. Decades later,
these grandiose gestures of brass-and-tympani extravagance
were read as the epitome of '70s bombast, self-mythologizing
elevations of rock and roll to Symphonic Spectacle, a fan-
blinding staging of Rock Gods, what critic Dave Marsh memo-
rably described as "pseudo events." The Rolling Stones would
have fun with such gestures, opening their 1975–76 American
and European tours with a snippet from Aaron Copland's
Fanfare for the Common Man, but Jagger's backstage smirk
is practically audible; you know that he's reveling in the self-
mocking, poking fun at the pretentiousness of Rock Shows.

In how much of his own grandiosity did Elvis have faith?
Maybe I even believed that he hummed Strauss to himself during Graceland mornings as a kind of heartfelt, if pompous,
soundtrack to his druggy days. Before intellect confused things,
before I learned Irony and Camp, I listened to the opening
of *Elvis: As Recorded at Madison Square Garden* and imagined The King backstage, waiting, elevating, testing his jumpsuit wings, larger than life as Strauss's octave-ambitious score
filled the venue and my head with pomp, my chest thumping
with Joy, Sunrise, Passion, Great Longing. Those musicians in
the dark must be pretty important to require such fanfare. I
believed. I was hooked. Though I can't listen to Elvis's entrance
anymore without a wry half-grin, I admit to loving its stirring
mock-seriousness no less now than I did when I was a kid in a

suburban basement ushered into spectacle, drifting without a guidebook somewhere between sincerity and satire.

"CERTAINLY RECORDED MUSIC haunts us almost by definition," says music critic Michelle Banks. "Technologies of recording allow the past to remain, to stay, and in some ways usurp and challenge the very usual and powerful notions of chronology; disembodied and nostalgic, recorded music perpetually carries with it both wanted and unwanted presences. And sometimes such presence can seem, at least for a moment and with varying levels of intensity, to occupy our whole bodies, our whole selves, metaphysically embodying blood for us. These are those songs that for whatever individual reasons, carry. They are the ones that take us back, pull us on, and rest waiting for us sometime again in the future."

I MEAN, I knew what "love" was. I loved my mom and dad, and my dog Molly, and my bike and cherry-coke Slurpees and baseball cards—so *I'm not in love* as a declaration resonated with me. I understood the negation there, maybe even the fear. But not much beyond the words' surface. The roads that led to puberty and the complications and losses beyond puberty were roads that 10cc showed me through the rec room stereo and the transistor radio at the Wheaton public pool. The haze of that melody filled my chest each time I listened and it was some-how meaningful, disturbed with presentiment, the singing and the arrangement, the graphic, major-minor mood changes—the poignant rainfall of those tear-jerking choral notes, and me—all inside a bright room Before Knowledge. What will I learn? That love is a tightening in the throat, love is expressed as dreams, love is a song on the radio.

And this: *big boys don't cry.* That sentence in the middle of the song (whispered by a receptionist at 10cc's Strawberry Studios in Cheshire, England, where the song was recorded) cut through the dreamy mystery, and chided me in a mother's disembodied voice. I was worrying about crying on the playground and in the classroom, and though that struggle was at times overwhelming, I sensed through the misery that there were larger complications looming, something unspecified yet fully felt in the grown-up singer's complexities, tensions that the music, in its twilit, atmospheric wash and yearning wordlessness, somehow defined for me.

Unburdened by taxonomy, we listen for the first time to a song as it says to us what it knows—in words we might soon sing along with, but also in chord changes, tempo shifts, eighth notes, in unseen sonic details that translate the calm or the bedlam of our inner lives—and when we listen as kids, when, after Mondrian, our minds haven't yet caught up with sensations, we trail the language and knowledge of songs wherever they take us.

Music enters us in many ways, through dreams, through spectacle. And through fear. The discordance of a record played at the wrong speed is different from the melancholy of, say, the Doppler effect, what Brian Wilson intuited and employed as the last, distressing noises at the end of *Pet Sounds*, the sounds of dejection and loss. Playing a record at the wrong speed was transgressive, hostile, chaotic in the ways that I'd imagined "bad trips" on LSD must have felt like, the inner horrors of disunities, of centers not holding, the stuff of nightmares. I didn't articulate to myself at the time that I didn't like, but that I also loved, that I could manipulate the turntable in such a way, let loose into stable suburbia a frightening new language that spoke of instability and disorientation. Rotating the RPM knob, sending my brother careening from the room, I turned music inside out, learning, without intending, the dark inside of a pop song. Another lesson at so many revolutions per minute.

SONIC BOY

*I*N OLD FRENCH it was an "emanation from the stars that acts upon one's character and destiny." In the 1300s, a "streaming ethereal power from the stars acting upon character or destiny of men." I'm peering into the oversized wooden console stereo in the family living room, watching a record turn under the weight of a tone arm and midrange stylus—roughly seven centuries later, star power of a different origin. The bulky silver knobs are within reach, the one that makes things shiny in my head, the one that fills my stomach with a weight I can't describe, the one that makes things too loud. Wes Montgomery's on, I think, or maybe George Shearing.

"C'MERE."

I'm in my older brother's bedroom. He's sat me down on his bed. Our parents are out of the house and he's inviting some friends over. "I just want to tell you. I'm probably going to get drunk tonight."

I stare blankly.

"Some friends—you know Tom and Pat from school?—and some other guys. They're coming over and we're gonna make some sloe gin fizzes. And we're gonna have fun and I'm probably gonna get drunk. So. Just letting you know. Keep it quiet." I'm already wondering what gin fizz is and what it looks like and what makes it slow.

Hours later and the rec room's pounding up through the bedroom floor. I sneak down the stairs of our split-level and gaze at a jumble of young guys and girls, some I know, some I don't, a smoky moving mass of bottoms and bell-bottoms and flannel. Everyone's holding glasses. Everyone's laughing. They're loud and talking to each other but I can't make out what they're saying. I don't want to stray much closer because I shouldn't be here, on the stairs, spying. *Boston*'s on and "More Than a Feeling" is playing—I know that one—and later, when I'm back in bed, "Peace of Mind" and "Foreplay/Long Time" and "Rock & Roll Band" and "Smokin'" and songs by other bands, muffled, score something I'm scared of and wonder about, those hands around the girls' hips, the leaping about, the leaning in, the smoking—if the songs make the guys do that or the other way around.

"INFLUENCE IS NOT influence. It's simply someone's idea going through my new mind." (Jean-Michel Basquiat)

I'D HEARD THAT Mike had gotten his hand down Mary's pants at a party in her basement, that her white jeans were on so tight that you could see the outline of his hand underneath. A week or so later I see him coming out of Kemp Mill Records clutching an album, that one with the bright primary-color paint splattered all over the cover. I want that.

RAISED AS AN only child, Kathryn Harrison grew up isolated, "the sole keeper" of her history. In "The Forest of Memory" she writes, of her past: "It is mine to do with what I will, to make sense of, perhaps, assembling the pieces into a coherent whole, a kind of narrative group portrait complete with background and foreground. Or to make into fiction, to invent a history that is possible, but untrue." Alone, she wonders:

> There is nothing that unfolded in the house of my child-hood that anyone can confirm, or deny. Countless trans-actions, most without consequence, but some fraught with significance—primal, formative, determinate—lack any witness other than myself. In the abstract, my being free of siblings, of parents, of anyone who might object to my dissembling, or even take note of an untruth, might provide me a tempting invitation to reinvent his-tory. But only in the abstract, only in theory. When I test the idea, contemplating how completely possible it is to rewrite my early years, it frightens me. What I feel isn't freedom but a freefall, and what could check the speed of my descent? Humans agree that what we call

"reality" depends on its being observed by at least one person. When a tree falls in my forest of memories and no one else hears it, has it happened? Is there a sound of one hand clapping?

Contemplating growing up without siblings? I might as well consider infinity. The history created by my four brothers, my sister, and me is rich and, as in every family, paradoxically commonplace and unprecedented: I am Me in large part because of Them, a random generation of closely related DNA gathering under the same roof.

Harrison's concerns originated in family chaos, dysfunction, and abandonment. Her anxieties looking back stem less from *How was I influenced?* than from *Who can corroborate me?* But I also wonder on the absence of older brothers or sisters and how I would've navigated such blankness, how it might've shaped me. Often I feel bad for those without older siblings, not because they were spared the teasing and scolding, but because the initiation into aesthetic pleasure and critical thinking can originate in accepting or rejecting the influences of an older brother or sister, or three. Such influence is a kind of weather through which you walk, daily, until, years later, you recognize what stuck to you, what you can't rub off, what you carry with you eternally. My brothers' musical tastes and my own, their soundtrack and mine, was a crucial threshold for me growing up. The anxiety of influence, writ domestic, circulating from bedroom to family room and back again.

JEAN PAUL GAULTIER: "Always my collections are made of different influences."

HARLEM, NEW YORK City, 1950s. A high school algebra teacher worries over the future of his younger brother Sonny, a restless kid with a criminal record who plays hard bebop, reveres Charlie "Bird" Parker, and has descended into the bedlam of West Village smack. Sonny can't see his older brother as anyone but an irritating, arbitrating guardian, a buttoned-up gatekeeper who refuses to listen to arguments from the other side because it's a hundred blocks south. Over the course of James Baldwin's masterful "Sonny's Blues," the narrator's harsh judgments of his brother soften, due in part to his grief over losing his own young daughter ("My trouble made his real," he acknowledges) and in part to a promise the narrator made to his mother. But mostly because of the surprising, redemptive power of art.

At the close of the story, the narrator, half-dubious, half-curious, agrees to go watch Sonny play at a club in the Village. Gazing at his brother at the piano and recognizing that the folks here aren't smacked-out degenerates but are kind intimates, treating Sonny warmly, as if he's family, as if he's at home, and then being forced to redefine what home means, the narrator is transformed. "All I know about music is that not many people ever really hear it," he admits. Stable, secure in the solve-for-x formulas of his vocation, though cripplingly grieving for his torn-asunder family, the narrator discovers in Sonny's environment a new appreciation for the discordant, improvisatory art form he'd scorned and willfully ignored, and for those inside it. The band's playing "Am I Blue?" and the narrator's under the influence:

> And even then, on the rare occasions when something opens within, and the music enters, what we mainly hear, or hear corroborated, are personal, private, vanishing evocations. But the man who creates the music is hearing something else, is dealing with the roar rising from the void and imposing order on it as it hits the air. What is evoked in him, then, is of another order, more terrible because it has no words, and triumphant, too, for that same reason. And his triumph, when he triumphs, is ours. I just watched Sonny's face.

"I DON'T BELIEVE in learning from other people's pictures," says Orson Welles. "I think you should learn from your own interior vision of things and discover, as I say, innocently, as though there had never been anybody."

MY BROTHERS JOHN, Jim, and Phil and my sister, Jane, were each born roughly a year apart from the other over a four-year span; I arrived four and a half years after my sister, so their intimate bunker mentality was forged in an era I didn't share. Leaving aside how this birth order may have shaped my independence or propensity toward seclusion, it certainly left me adrift on my own quiet island of musical taste—though their obsessions were on the horizon, near. Yes; Emerson, Lake & Palmer; the Eagles; *Switched-On Bach*; Grateful Dead; *Tubular Bells*; Elton John; Crosby, Stills, Nash & Young; America— these were in high rotation on the family stereo as I was growing up and tuning in. That you'll find few of these albums in my collection now doesn't mean they haven't been imprinted in me.

Their tastes in music were, as mine were, informed by Casey Kasem's weekly Top 40 show broadcast on WPGC 95.5 FM in Washington D.C., and by magazines, late-night television, and the singles and albums that their friends, and friends of their friends, possessed. "One father is more than a hundred schoolmasters," says George Herbert. But what about five siblings? Having older brothers and a sister guaranteed that as a kid I'd at least have an ear to the door of a room where songs about fucking or drinking or Satan weren't whispered about in code on the playground at school but gossiped about openly, if often naively.

One particularly potent source of gossip was Billy Joel's "Only the Good Die Young," from his 1977 album *The Stranger*. My siblings and I attended Catholic schools from first grade through high school, and the education we received in the church and in classrooms informed our daily lives, from wake to sleep, from the songs we listened to on the radio and on albums to the movies we hoped to see. When I wanted to see a new release, my parents would consult the *Catholic Standard*, the weekly Roman Catholic archdiocese of Washington D.C.'s official newspaper that materialized on our kitchen table with solemn regularity. The editors at the Catholic News Service classified each new movie with a letter rating reflecting the movie's morality and intended audience, from A-I for general patronage, to L for a limited adult audience, to O—the letter I'd both dread seeing and thrill to—for morally offensive. As I recall, these ratings were fairly ironclad in the house; my mom had great faith in the *Standard*'s standards, and though the ratings were meant as a guide, we lived by them.

Into this landed an uninvited guest. Released as a single, "Only the Good Die Young" was, I quickly discovered, anti-Catholic. More specifically it was a paean to getting up a good girl's skirt. I'd learn much later that the Catholic Church–affiliated campus radio station at Seton Hall University had banned the song for its satiric lyrics hostile to spiritual purity, sexual chastity, and church teachings. Other less-secular-leaning stations had joined the protest, and soon the song reaped the predictable rewards of infamy: it rocketed up the *Billboard* Hot 100 singles chart, peaking at number twenty-four.

"You Catholic girls start much too late," Joel sang, and though I was a bit young to get it, I got it, especially as the song became incendiary under my parents' watchful eyes. I think Jim had bought the album, but I believe we weren't allowed to play it in the house—or at any rate we were strongly discouraged. But I heard it: when my brothers' friends would come over to play it out of range of my parents; I heard it on the radio; mostly I heard it in my head when at night in bed I'd score the changing postures of the girls at school from playful to assertive, virginal to whatever-was-next, the glowing horizon of bras and underwear, romance and sex, just there and just out of reach. The panting insistence in Joel's song—which he wrote about a crush on a girl in high school back at Levittown, Long Island, where he grew up—was a murky language to me, but one it seemed that my older siblings were speaking already, or knew enough stray words of to claim as their own. Joel smirks: "I might as well be the one." *To do what?* I wondered. My siblings were closer than I was to understanding, to dealing with the song's winking *carpe diem*, and this glaring distance between them and me hurt, producing a chest-tightening anxiety that I'd never catch up with them.

THE CHANGE HAPPENS before you're aware of it. At the public pool I'd been underwater in the shallow end, looking through giant goggles at undulating legs and arms and hips, a world that looked like the one up on the pool deck, but strange, surreally quiet but for muffled laughter and the unfathomable sentences spoken in the air above my head. A few minutes later, absorbed, I'm watching the leaves stuck in the drain and look up to see my sister and brothers turning away. Hues Corporation's "Rock the Boat" or Wings's "Listen to What the Man Said" is playing on the radio next to you, and that's it: a moment is scored.

Black-light posters, harmonies, hormones, songs behind closed doors: these are the moving parts of the time machine your older siblings constructed. I go back to an era when their albums and the overheard conversations about them were tantalizing, alluring signposts for a future I'd yet to comprehend, a blurry place where my sister's face changed from innocent to complicated as she listened to James Taylor or yelled, "Firehouse! Whoo!" with our Kiss *Alive!* album or sang along to Elton John belting out "bitch!" Here's what I remember: when her boyfriend broke up with her following a mammoth, silencing snow that had fallen all over the eastern seaboard, she joined us in the front yard, wiping away tears and half-confidently, half-morosely grabbing a shovel to help, re-entering her changed world. I wonder now what song she'd listened to that night, or that morning in her heartache. I know her album collection, and so I could guess. When the decade tripped dangerously into its last couple of years and into the next and Phil started bringing home Sex Pistols, Ramones, Jam, and Clash records, I heard them with the same ferocity he did—only I couldn't yet avail myself of the world outside of our house as he and his friends did so freely, donning vintage thrift-shop suit jackets and skinny ties, drinking, driving, turning up the car stereo, eyeing the New Wave chicks, sniffing the air for mayhem and anarchy.

ONE MORNING SOMETIME in the late 1970s, I staggered into the kitchen where my family, in ones and twos, sat for breakfast, and announced that I'd listened in the middle of the night as DC101 played Boston's "Don't Look Back" into Led Zeppelin's "Stairway to Heaven" and that I now understood the meaning of life. I hope my siblings laughed at me. I'm sure they did.

ATHENS, OHIO. FIRST Street. My neighbor and some friends of hers are out on her front porch. I walk past and hear a song coming from their house that I've never heard before, and can't place. In the few moments it takes to reach my front steps the music seems to have moved from sweet to ferocious to anthemic to desolate and back again. The singer's great. The riffs are loud, but clean. "Who *is* that?" I yell from the street.

She smiles beatifically at me. "It's Nirvana!"

When *Nevermind* was released in the fall of 1991 I was only vaguely aware of Kurt Cobain's band. I'd looked the other way when their early Sub Pop records were issued, as I hadn't been ready yet for their tuneful howl. What I heard my neighbor say was "nirvana" with a lowercase *n*. In the way we instantaneously make sense of a complex moment and its scope, it felt like what she had described for me was a feeling, a place, made of roar and stillness, to where she'd been transported, a spiritual instant. Not much later, when Nirvana took off commercially, I made the critical appellative correction, but the influential exchange on the street had imprinted itself in me. That was less music I heard walking by her porch on an ordinary sunny day in autumn than a state of being.

The summer between my junior and senior years at the University of Maryland I took on a three-hour weekly summer show at WMUC 88.1 FM, the campus radio station. I'd be playing jazz. I'd had a rock-and-roll show for a couple of years already and was steadily moving beyond the post-midnight graveyard shifts, when Dave, the music director, asked if I'd consider the summer gig. I'd little experience with jazz music, but I said, *Yeah*.

Or maybe I'd requested the show. I'm somewhat baffled by the whole blurry episode now, considering just how green I was, my "taste in jazz" having been informed only by the Dave Brubeck records my dad had bought in the 1950s and often played in the house while we were growing up. Later there was George Shearing, Al Hirt, a Wes Montgomery LP or two—but no Dizzy, no Coltrane, no Parker, no Miles. Nothing on Blue Note, nothing on Savoy.

Rather, I'd tune in daily, fanatically, to the now-defunct WHFS free-form music station housed for many years at 102.3

FM in Bethesda, Maryland, and later at 99.1 in Annapolis, an unprecedented, twenty-four-hour education in vernacular rock-and-roll history. My favorite DJ there was Jonathan Gilbert, aka Weasel, who had the late-afternoon shift, and whose late-Friday sets I'd listen to, master classes in selecting, pacing, and celebrating songs that celebrated the weekend and all of the liberating promises music makes. There were other great DJs there—among them "Cerphe," Milo, Meg, Adele Abrams, Susan Desmarais on the weekends, the laconic Bob, or "Bob Here"—but Weasel, a chirpy-voiced music maniac gifted with an encyclopedic knowledge of rock and roll, a love of both the cheery AM-radio-era singles format and seldom-played R&B, New Wave, Punk, and alternative album deep cuts, and a quick-fire wit, was essential, a lifetime curator of my taste. Occasionally I'd wander onto local country and blues radio stations, too, and on some gray, tiring drives home after classes, up slushy, heavily trafficked University Boulevard, past strip malls and low, beaten-down red-brick garden apartments, I'd tune in to WPFW at 89.3 FM, the Washington D.C. jazz station, and listen under cloudy skies to a foreign tongue.

My JAZZ INFLUENCES were mostly imagined. Those songs I'd listen to while driving—propulsive yet seemingly formless, lengthy, difficult to my untutored ear—made me think of the insides of the wealthy homes and apartments on upper

Connecticut Avenue or Georgetown in Washington D.C., lived in by the kinds of people who I imagined listened to jazz music rather than to, say, the Dead Kennedys or New Order. Red wine, walls of bookshelves, dimmed reading lamps, *New Yorker* magazines, multi-course suppers. The rich, urban voices of the male and female DJs spoke for these cardboard cutouts that I'd placed in sophisticated, unassailable environments; they were older, smarter, more dimensional than I. These images had to come from somewhere. Perhaps stray glimpses from movies, television shows, a friend's father's den, an ad in a magazine gathered in my brainpan over time to narrate a story that never occurred. I'm fascinated by the way the imagination stages a dynamic set with so few resources: when I read the opening sentence of any account, fictional or otherwise, I instantly picture the protagonist; yet how do I do this when the sentence is merely "He arrived at midnight" or "She walked into the bedroom"? I wonder which "she" it is that I imagine, and why her. And if she's wholly imagined, where do I get the parts to assemble her? When presented with little more than a silhouette, we grab the nearest brush and palette we can find, and go to work filling in. Alone in our heads, intuitive, without the tutelage of siblings or friends, I wonder what influence we are under then.

I THREW DARTS. I began my first set with Brubeck's "Balcony Rock" from my dad's scratchy *Jazz Goes to College* album. (I hear the opening notes now as I write.) While the song played

I'd grab from the overstuffed jazz shelf any album that looked similar in vintage—cover graphics that weren't too far-out or contemporary, say—placed it on the other turntable, dropped the needle, and listened through headphones. If the song fit in tone or mood, or at least shared a similar time signature, I'd cue it up. Most of the cuts I played were long, so I had plenty of time to explore unfamiliar albums while I was broadcasting. I was acquainted with the names of—maybe—a third of the artists I'd play. The experience was utterly thrilling. Unable to lead with any substantial knowledge of jazz history or musicians, influenced by what I imagined a jazz show should sound like, haphazardly matching the aesthetics of sleeve art or record labels or the size of the band, I led with intuition and wild surmise, leaping across decades and styles and trends, Louie to Chick to Herbie to Monk and back again.

I'd named my regular radio show "Innocent Startings," reflecting my then-obsession with Colin MacInnes's novel *Absolute Beginners*, and this show I dubbed "Innocently Jazz Startings," proceeding in my mash-up to go blind and trust hunches. Undoubtedly I insulted the intelligence of the one or two genuine jazz fans among the dozen listening to my show on campus or on the fringes of the College Park, Berwyn Heights, and Greenbelt neighborhoods where the fifteen-watt signal struggled to penetrate. My sets were ersatz, and tacky maybe, certainly naive and unlearned—and yet I trusted that the linkages among eras and expressions, the transitions among unfamiliar songs, might cohere. More knowledgeable about jazz now, I'd probably be embarrassed by the set lists, if I could locate them. I might have a cassette of one of the shows down-stairs, but I'd rather not know. I'm going to believe that, conjur-ing influences on the fly, improvising, I made something whole.

"ROCK AND ROLL might not solve your problems, but it does let you dance all over them."

That's Pete Townshend. I don't remember when I read the quote but it stuck, is reaffirmed at every sweaty show I enjoy or lonely night with tunes I endure. (Today's show-and-tell example courtesy of shuffle play is the Monkees' terrific "Tear Drop City." *About as low as I've felt in a long time*, the singer laments, but good luck keeping still while you sympathize with him.) Townshend also observed that "rock and roll is fun songs about sad stuff." At least I'd always thought he'd said that; I've since seen it attributed only to the novelist Mary Jo Parker. In the flux of influences I give this truism—borne out in my music collection, within sorry relationships, and on long, aimless drives—to Townshend, a man I'll never meet yet will always trust. Anyway, it's in the air above my head and under my moving feet now, eternally, whoever said it.

AT SAINT ANDREW the Apostle, a local rock group is plugged in. It's the early 1970s and I'm sitting with dozens of other seven- or eight-year-olds on the cold floor of the All-Purpose

Room across from the principal's office and the bathrooms. I'm looking at the three grown-up men in front of me and their girlish, shaggy hair, tight striped pants, red and purple shirts and ruffles, their bright white smiles. This power trio had been invited to play at school, men with guitars and amps among the nuns and lay faculty. I don't know why they're here beyond the novel entertainment value; through the fog of memory one of them's talking about safety, about getting out of your bedroom window in case of a fire? Or is he talking about polluting, and not to do that? Some of the girls are sighing; many are smiling and giggling with each other. The amplification cuts through the blur and I'm there, just down the hall from church, darkened now at midweek, scared of and enthralled by the tiny amps and the sudden huge noise they make, the immediate *thing* in my head of physical sound, the glossy treble up into my sinuses and sparking behind my eyes, and a hand on—*in*—my chest. I'm a sonic boy.

FANTASY PARK

O N MEMORIAL DAY weekend in 1975, a Washington D.C. radio station—I think it was DC101—broadcast "The Beatles at Fantasy Park," syndicated over two hundred stations. Hipped to the event by my older brother, I was primed. We recorded the entire broadcast over two Certron 90-minute cassette tapes that we'd bought at Dart Drug. The "concert" was, of course, bogus, a crass hallmark of the era's propensity for pseudo-events, and of the timeless desire for the Beatles to reunite. The show's creators played a set list of Beatles songs onto which they dubbed arena-sized concert clamor: a roaring, elated crowd; ambient spectator chatter caught on-mike; interviews with local personalities and with the individual Beatles themselves (actors wrestling with Liverpool accents); reporters offering remote, on-the-spot features inside of the venue. An exciting Concert Event, indeed.

The verisimilitude was astounding. More than four decades later I remember the top-of-the-head-coming-off thrill I experienced that my words now can only pretend to translate. It was the coolest thing that I'd ever heard, magical, strange—even though I knew it was a faked event—a conflation of dreams and technology, most of this beyond my articulation at the time. I remember the realistic-sounding jostling of the reporters as they got closer to Lennon or Harrison, who were opining for a group of journalists backstage. I remember marveling at the hoots and cheers and whistles of the crowd, the levels of which was expertly raised and lowered during the performance. I remember that the show's creators decided to open with "Baby, You're a Rich Man," which was a weird-enough choice that my brothers and I debated it for days afterward. There was definitively something of the era in the whole event: our family had bought the "Red" and "Blue" albums at Korvettes a couple of years before, and my head tingled with imagined scenes of this concert, and at the very real delight of the idea of the Beatles back together, manufactured and canned as the whole thing was.

A few years later, a rumor was floated that the Beatles were reuniting to play a series of benefit concerts for the Cambodian and Vietnamese boat people. That morning at the kitchen table I hopefully clipped the article from the *Washington Post* and, up in my bedroom, handled it as if it were a sacred text. The rumor burned up the playground at Saint Andrew the Apostle for a few days and, like the fade of the imagined crowd after the last encore at Fantasy Park, soon disappeared for good. The 1980s and Lennon's murder were around the corner.

I have the "Fantasy Park" cassette tapes downstairs in the basement, somewhere. I'm hesitant to dig them out and play them. My tape deck has lurked down there for years now, as well; I'm not sure I'd remember how to hook it up to my stereo. Also, I'm wary of the brittle tapes themselves coming apart in a cloud of dust if I did try to play them.

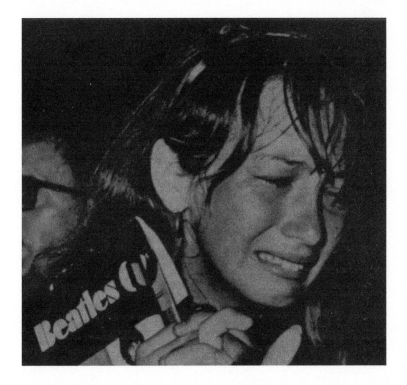

I FIRST SAW her in the mid-1970s, in a coffee-table book. She's at a Beatles show in Philadelphia, August 1966. The world of stories this girl spun for me. I'd love to know who and where she is now. But part of me is skeptical of that impulse, happy to let her live in my imagination. There she's less a teen-age girl in perpetuity—that kind of embalming doesn't inter-est me—than a human possessed beyond language. An endless source of inquiry. "Human faces," said Henri Cartier-Bresson, "are such a world!"

An image seduces us into believing that a moment is eter-nal, that we can dwell in a fraction of time and believe that that instant has currency and value in the future. Photos are, of course, liars. Vittorio Canta, a painter, said, "Cameras that capture the moment are giving us the impression to own it." After the forty-minute show, she dried her eyes and under-arms, went home with her ears ringing, singing, wrote in her diary, exclaimed to her girlfriends on the phone or in school the next day, *the Beatles grew mustaches*. But here she's stilled. Her expression, its blend of joy and anguish, bliss and bur-den frightened me. Whatever knowledge and language I might attain would take years to catch up with the sensation.

I saw the photo before I understood that overwhelming pleasure and surprising release can terrify. This Beatles Girl will always live in my imagination as a source of unease, dissolving my rational attempts to make sense of her. She's having fun, right? She's not unhappy, right? The grainy black-and-white secures her in a past beyond my reach, so I can't ask her, Why do you look this way? I wonder. What does she remember of that concert? This girl remains unknowable to me, and for that I can't relinquish her.

As I sat in my basement with *The Beatles: An Illustrated Record*, written and compiled by U.K. journalists Roy Carr and Tony Tyler, she was living out for me a story that she has no say in, complicating my naive understanding of girlish expressions around me at St. Andrew the Apostle. Like a transparency, I held the afterimage of Beatles Girl up to those faces and wondered if they'd match. I did see something similar in the girls on the blacktop: torment when they were upset, their faces red and streaming tears. But never when they were joyous, their hair lifting on the swing set, laughter in the air.

Beatles Girl obscured things. In her face, delight and anguish meet and collapse. The only language I have to describe it is approximate. Words like *bittersweet*. Or that her face shows a depth of experience. A potent blend of suffering and ecstasy, nearly saintly, beatific. Something I couldn't name then but I can now. Surrender.

THE "FANTASY PARK" tapes are a locus for a strange, dark memory. Weeks after my brothers and I recorded the event, I was down in the basement listening to the tapes obsessively. Something overtook me and, out of body, I watched as my finger pressed the red RECORD button on the tape recorder, erasing several seconds. I stared at the recorder, dumbstruck. I was heartsick. My heart raced, I depressed the button again, and again, alone in the basement, I erased more of the show. It was bizarre, and kind of sick. I knew that I'd deeply regret doing it—and I still do, these many years later—and yet in the moment I got off on a kind of power that I could lord over myself. *Don't*, I said. *Do it*, I said. *Don't!* I did. I was nauseated, ashamed of the disappointment I'd created for my brothers who also liked listening to the tapes, and was ashamed of myself, and yet I luxuriated, unhappily, in a quasi-masochistic drama with only myself to blame, myself to champion. The songs were permanently interrupted by the quiet of the basement and my own stupid breathing. I was learning without realizing the ways we can surrender to an unhappy impulse, betray ourselves against our will, often with malice, and often with heartbreak. (President Nixon had resigned less than a year before my trivial transgression in the basement, the infamous eighteen-and-a-half-second gap in the Watergate audiotape soon to surface. Now, I associate those two erasures in my memory, impossibly, frivolously.) I'll never get those seconds back.

What's been erased has been imprinted in me in a different, equally unchangeable way. The uneasy, urgent blend of excitement, fear, regret, and power I felt in those moments was curious and wretched.

HOLD YOUR PHONE TO THIS
ESSAY AND SELECT TAG NOW

"THE IDEA STARTED when one of the company's founders wanted to be able to identify a particular guitar riff and thought there would be value in creating an algorithm that could identify music that was sung or hummed. Soon thereafter, that idea merged with the concept of creating technology that could identify recorded music. Today, SoundHound is about enabling people around the world to identify any type of sound, whether it's created originally or recorded." (Katie McMahon, Vice President of Sales and Marketing, SoundHound, April 9, 2013)

AROUND THE TIME of *The Mary Tyler Moore Show*'s final episode, in March of 1977, I was hanging out with one of my older brothers in our driveway. I loved the show's theme song, especially the little drum fill in the opening bars before the proper melody begins. I used to hum the song to myself on the way to school and back, out playing in the yard or on my bike, *dumm*-ing da-*dumm*-ing that cool drum part out loud. One day it occurred to me that I was going to hear that theme for the last time in my life. This was one of the first instances as a kid when I was confronted with irreplaceable loss—goldfish renewed themselves with a visit to the pet store; flat tires were plumped with air; my best friend Karl had moved away three years earlier, but we kept up with letters. This drum fill was going to simply vanish, never to be heard again, destined to live on only in the melancholy needle-drops of memory. I told my brother that I could barely wait to hear the theme for the last time. He told me that he was going to talk out loud over that part so that I'd miss it.

"THE IMPLICATIONS ARE overwhelmingly positive. Users want that instant gratification of being able to identify a song they hear and like, whether they are in their car, a bar, a sports stadium, etc. And with SoundHound, that's exactly what they get. Moreover, the rich feature set including LiveLryics—another SoundHound Inc.–created technology—has the impact of reinvigorating the love of lyrics and helps anyone who wants to learn the words of a song. Our fans have told us that SoundHound LiveLyrics are to aspiring singers what Guitar Hero is to the aspiring guitarist." (McMahon)

THE AGONY! (My brother knew what he was doing.) If he talked over the song so I couldn't hear it, that meant that I'd already heard it for the last time. I can't remember whether or not my brother did what he promised. Dali: "The difference between false memories and true ones is the same as for jewels: it is always the false ones that look the most real, the most brilliant." This gem—whether or not a brother was unkind—I've lost for good.

"APPLICATIONS LIKE SOUNDHOUND not only help people discover and share new music but, in many ways, they also help reacquaint users with music from earlier times in their lives. Many SoundHounders use the app to capture a song they may not have heard for several years but now want to add it to their playlist or listen to it, buy or stream the track. So it is also a tool that aids in memory and reminiscence." (McMahon)

PLUTARCH WROTE "CONSOLATION to His Wife" in the first century, when he and his spouse, separated by many miles, were awash in the grief of losing their small child. They bore weeks apart as their letters to each other slowly, agonizingly arrived, each missive weighted with anticipation and desire, love and loneliness. "The messenger you sent with tidings of the death of our little daughter apparently missed me on his road to Athens, and consequently I learned about the child only when I arrived in Tanagra," Plutarch writes, adding: "I suppose that the funeral has already taken place." Imagine such an interval.

"MUSIC IS OFTEN associated with specific moments and memories, and technologies like SoundHound and the feature set provide a way for users to capture, catalogue, and create music memories that live onward and can have interactions that go beyond the moment in time." (McMahon)

WITHIN MONTHS OF *The Mary Tyler Moore Show*'s final airing, the sitcom began invading our sunny afternoons; at one point, channel 5, the Washington D.C. NBC affiliate station, was airing up to three episodes in a row in the daytime, under clustered themes such as "Lou's Lu-Lu's!" But at that age I didn't really understand reruns, where they came from, who was in charge of them, why they happened—*if* they'd happen— except that *Get Smart* and *My Three Sons* were great and we were blessed when they were beamed into our rec rooms every afternoon, those broadcasts originating from faraway Baltimore caught, tenuously, by a movable antenna on our roof that we activated from a console atop our TV set. I pictured the antenna rotating slowly toward invisible radio waves.

"SOUNDHOUND MAKES IT possible for people to discover, enjoy, and share new music almost instantaneously. This is a dramatic change from the days of having to wait for a song on the radio to end in the hopes the on-air DJ will broadcast the name of the song and artist. At the same time, the wholly unique feature of Sing/Hum recognition may have impact that spurs people to test their ability to process what they have previously heard and provide their own rendition in attempt to have it matched against SoundHound." (McMahon)

"As one might expect, the Yeah Yeah Yeahs have a zero-tolerance policy when it comes to fans ruining the show for other fans by insisting on watching the entire performance in the glowing light of their smartphone screens.

"Ahead of a recent show at Webster Hall, the trio posted a sign up front urging fans to ditch their 'smart devices' in favor of a more intelligent show-viewing experience.

"'PLEASE DO NOT WATCH THE SHOW THROUGH A SCREEN ON YOUR SMART DEVICE/CAMERA,' read the literal sign-of-the-times. 'PUT THAT SHIT AWAY as a courtesy to the person behind you and to Nick, Karen, and Brian. MUCH LOVE AND MANY THANKS! YEAH YEAH YEAHS.'

"According to a *SPIN* magazine staffer who was at the show, vocalist Karen O vocalized the appeal near the start of the set by allowing the audience to take photos for a few minutes, before instructing them to 'put those motherfuckers away.'" (*Gawker*, April 8, 2013)

"Since its beginning, Shazam believed in leveraging the power of mobile technology to enable music discovery because mobile goes with you, wherever you are, whether you're in a quiet coffee shop or a noisy club. In a lot of ways, it was an idea and a technology that was almost a decade ahead of its time. When Shazam launched, all people had to do was dial 2580 on their phone and Shazam would send an SMS text message of the song name and artist. With the release of Shazam as an app in 2008, it became even easier—now, all people have to do is open Shazam and point it to the music playing to get the song and artist, album artwork, links to YouTube, and social sharing with Facebook and Twitter." (Will Mills, Vice President of Music and Content, Shazam, June 9, 2013)

"MAN IS AN imagining being." (Gaston Bachelard)

YOUNG CAUCASIANS HAD played, I think. The 9:30 Club in Washington D.C. was at its dark, sweaty best. I was with friends, but at the end of the night my circle of buddies had dissolved in that wonderfully messy way that things dissolve in your twenties, friends vanishing, friendly strangers materializing, values morphing in the smoke, the boundaries among intimates stretching, redefining with each beer, each snort of coke, each band, your ringing ears scoring it all. Startlingly, the person standing next to me as the show closed down was a girl from one of my classes, a cute blonde I'd had some conversations with in the classroom. She turned to me after the last song, looked directly in my eyes, cupped my cheek with her soft hand, and sighed. She turned, left, and vanished.

"SINCE ITS LAUNCH in iTunes, Shazam has been one of the apps that people love to show off to their friends, which is why its growth has been driven primarily by word of mouth rather than marketing. The service helps people quickly and easily discover the music they like, then go on to purchase it, which benefits them as well as supports the music industry in general. In fact, Shazam drives more than $300 million in digital music sales–that's 10 percent of global music sales. Additionally, people can easily share their finds with friends—they don't need to hum the song or remember the lyrics—they can simply share their tag on Facebook or Twitter." (Mills)

MY BOYISH WAITING for the afternoon reruns of *The Mary Tyler Moore Show* involved . . . well, waiting. We're aware at the hyper speed by which we live our lives: when virtually anything happens now in, say, the remote countryside of France, or in Iraq, I can know about it within seconds. This is staggering news. This is, also, not news. Lamenting the light-speed of culture is already a dated complaint, fading in the bright gleam of new and wonderful technological advances.

"SHAZAM IS AN established verb now, with many other companies describing themselves as the 'Shazam for real estate,' etc., and this mindshare and market dominance in music and now TV and advertising is something we're very proud of. As Shazam evolves expect more that future generations can do with

music and media you've engaged with on our service. Shazam
has certainly helped break artists at a faster pace than previously and has also helped artists who could have previously not
got a large audience, get traction." (Mills)

WE RENTED A car recently to drive from Illinois to Maryland
to visit family. The vehicle came equipped with satellite radio.
We tentatively played around with the radio during the opening
leg of the trip, at first overwhelmed, then amused, by the range
of station choices: '60s on 6, '70s on 7, '80s on 8. All Elvis, All
Day? Broadcast poolside from Graceland? Yes, please. But we
were soon disappointed by the numbingly repeated songs and the
innumerable commercials. Ditto with All Sinatra, All the Time.

It didn't take long for me to remember that there are major-
league-baseball stations on satellite radio. Having access to
every game played that day and night filled me with head-
lifting joy. I switched among games being played on the East
Coast and in the Midwest, learned what West Coast matchups I
could anticipate listening to tonight if we were still driving, our
headlights boring bright holes in the dark. Home announcers,
regional commercials, dozens of games, hundreds and hundreds
of plays described, visualized.

I didn't anticipate that, oddly, I'd miss the vanishing of a
radio signal as we went through the tunnel in the Allegheny
Mountains, the game's reception drifting away as we drove on,

static interrupting the announcers, their voices adrift in white noise, the game left to be played in my imagination, the inning truncated by geography and signal range now a transparency draped over memories of another game, and still another, infinite layers of recollections and affection originating in loss—until the present voices resume as we leave the tunnel. There are two outs now.

"I KNOW."

"Killer song."

"I can't remember what album it's on, the first one? That doesn't sound right."

"Can't remember."

"I think."

We look down at our phones, sitting dark on the table.

. . .

"Oh man, cool song."

"What is it? I can't make it out."

"You know, it's . . . fuck, what's his name. God, I can picture him. Can't remember. Anyway. Awesome song."

"Oh right, I think I know this." I look at the speakers. "Is it the jukebox?"

"No, it's a mix CD at the bar, I think. Jukebox's busted."

We glance at the bartender who's solo, and harried, serving patrons three deep. We look down at our phones.

"SHAZAM HAS FUNDAMENTALLY democratized music discovery and empowered hundreds of millions of people to engage with any music whenever and wherever they hear it. There are very few people if no one on earth who could recognize the huge volume and variety of music that Shazam can. This is a seismic shift that has invented a new category of consumer behavior not only with music, but also with television (primarily with people Shazam'ing their TV to engage with the music) and evolving beyond this at pace." (Mills)

KATE WAS DATING another DJ at WMUC, the University of Maryland campus radio station where, as a senior, I had a coveted Friday afternoon, three-to-six shift. She called the studio during my show and asked if I wanted to hang out afterward at Town Hall, a gray-cement townie bar on Route One. I had a girlfriend but a secret crush on Kate, who had long stick-straight reddish-brown hair and didn't wear much makeup. She was a painting major. Her nose was nice, probably too large to her, and her eyes were blue and active. She was quiet, but dry and cynical. She was cigarette-y and sexy. I said sure. A couple of hours later over pitchers of beers she shared stories of growing up in nearby Greenbelt, of living in a lower-middle-class family, of struggles and low ceilings in a concrete suburbia. Neither of us mentioned our significant others as we got very drunk and smoked and laughed. I drove her home and we parked in front of her house and made out for hours while the oldies station played on the car radio. Several times we got close to pushing beyond what either of us was actually ready for, and cooled off and de-fogged the windshield by pulling away, joking, listening to the radio, to Chuck Berry and the Four Seasons and Freddy "Boom Boom" Cannon and the Everly Brothers and Stax and Motown. She rolled her eyes at the corny songs, sang along to the Four Tops, and for several minutes essayed the Drifters' "Up on the Roof" as a coded paean to teenage suicide. At that time, in that place, with my hands around her waist and her taste on my lips, her theory seemed novel, and brilliant. We fooled around some more and the car battery died. Neither of us had money or the wherewithal to secure a tow truck, so she invited me to spend the night on her bedroom floor. She came out of her bathroom wearing pajamas, smelling of Marlboros and Colgate, and smiling sheepishly. I slept on the floor next to her bed. I was in the bedroom of a girl I didn't know. The next morning she asked me for ten dollars.

A COUPLE OF weeks later, I drove slowly past Kate's house, then hit I-495, the Beltway through Maryland and Virginia, and for a couple of hours circled Washington D.C., drinking a six-pack of Schaefer, listening to the oldies station. The songs that night scored a pathetic evening of remorse and lurid imagination, singing in pop changes a story I made up and made

myself believe, of acting nobly, charitably, ignoring the truths
that every other song dangerously skirted. That playlist is long
gone, irreplaceable, broadcast through night air from some
remote place. For those aimless hours, no other arrangement
of tunes could have mattered, could have approached the song-
book of twenty-something sorrow they achieved as I dipped
in and out of music, loudly singing along to songs I couldn't
replay, believing their promises and then bitterly denouncing
them, and drove around and around. Kate's body and voice,
the songs that reshaped them, ghosted the car. The music was
intense in its presentness, issuing from speakers and leaking
out of windows, and trailing me like exhaust. That they were
here and gone—in the car with me, then not—only made the
heartbreak of their arrival, full of promises and good times,
worse. Or, sweeter. These songs weren't in my pocket. They
were gone.

I stored that drive's soundtrack in my head for a long time,
played it on occasion, as if rifling through a box of 45s, but
the list grew and shrank, had songs added, deleted. Songs disappeared. My imagination stoked that night's playlist the way
memory required. In this century, I could've aimed my phone
at the car speakers, ID'd each song, posted them as wretched
updates to Facebook, had a real-time curating of a sad and solitary night. Now it feels as if loss is replaced instantly by every-
thingness. Which document is greater, I wonder, which more
lasting? Memory's shape-shifting hard drive, or the humming

circuits of my iPhone? I'm skeptical in each direction; my answer lies somewhere in the middle.

"How much of human life is lost in waiting." (Ralph Waldo Emerson)

Digital-photography apps like Hipstamatic and Instagram offer lenses and film stock that promise a kind of Instant Nostalgia, a way to frame the present moment as if it's come to us from the past and thus weighted with value, having endured the long, emotional journey from then to now. Snapchat seems to want to go the other way, to offer a digital simulation of perishability. This app will reverse the infinity vortex of the Internet. Imagine throwing that shoebox stuffed with Polaroids into the fire, scattering your love letters in the river, deleting the past with impunity, leaving no traces. Anti-Save. This image will vanish in seconds.

"To use Snapchat, you download the Apple or Android app, find your contacts, and start taking photos or videos. You determine how long they can be viewed—from one to ten seconds.

"The 'snaps' are then deleted from Snapchat servers. But that doesn't mean they always disappear. A recipient can take a screen shot, saving it forever, if they like. Other workarounds have also popped up on the Web.

"YouTube is full of videos of Snapchat users making quick, funny faces. There's also a not-suitable-for-work Facebook page called 'Snapchat Nudes.'

"[Snapchat CEO Evan] Spiegel insists his service isn't all about sex. Mention Snapchat to consumers, and teens and young adults light up.

"Jennifer Yvette Leiva of Anaheim, California, enjoys it for the timed photos. 'You like to goof around and not have people throw the pictures back in your face,' she says.

"'It's an easy way to keep in touch with your friends,' says Brooke Bower of San Diego." ("Snapchat's Young Audience Fuels a Growth Streak," *USA Today*, June 5, 2013)

BUT WHAT'S REALLY gone for good? "Yet Another Way to Retrieve Deleted Snapchat Photos." (*Salon.com*, June 4, 2013)

IN JUNE OF 2001, I traveled with the Fleshtones on a five-city tour of the Midwest. In Cleveland, I woke up on the floor of the promoter's house, a large, three-story lakeside home caked with matted cat hair. I was tired and hungover. Bleary-eyed, I glanced across the room and saw singer Peter Zaremba lying on a ratty couch. He stretched and looked miserable. "I'm too old for this shit," he said, as much to himself as to me.

An hour later in the living room our little kit bags are packed and we're set to say thanks to our hosts and pile back into the crowded van—when the quiet is assaulted by a loud song someone put on the turntable. Its anthemic rush and sixteenth notes knife through my hangover. Within a minute I feel jolted awake. By the end of the number, I feel redeemed. *Who is this?*

"Detroit Cobras," the bass player Ken Fox said, reading my mind. "It's an old Mickey Lee Lane tune. They call it 'Hey Sailor.' We just called it 'Hey Sah-Lo-Ney' when we did it."

Into the van we went. We headed south toward Columbus on the gray interstate in front of menacing storm clouds, and I played and replayed the song in my head, its B-12 sonic boost still coursing through my sorry veins. I had to hear that song again. I knew I would within a few days, maybe even later that night. The wait felt Biblical.

"DON'T PLAY WHAT'S there, play what's not there." (Miles Davis)

THE IPOD HAS fundamentally changed listening to music while traveling. Before, on road trips, I'd have to bring along a clumsy, oversized wallet stuffed with CDs; halfway through the drive I'd invariably regret not bringing, say, the *Pow City!* compilation when on I-80 I craved Johnny Jones & The King Casuals' "It's Gonna Be Good." As of this writing, I have over twenty-three thousand songs on my iPod, from the A-Bones to ZZ Top. I'd have to drive fifty days consecutively, twenty-four hours a day, in order to listen to every song. This is an absurdly wonderful idea.

Yet, here are my Old Man Shakes Fist At iCloud questions: do I love more a song that I have to wait to posses? Do I care more for the eBay-won 45 that took ten days to arrive in my mailbox than for the mp3 acquired in moments?

"PEOPLE USE SHAZAM to help build the soundtrack of their lives. And by having the music recognized by our service, that creates something that was previously ephemeral in your mind as a memory, and puts this as a quantifiable result into the device you spend most time with. And not only does this then frictionlessly allow you to purchase that music (further cementing your relationship with the music you might have not heard again), but also share this memory with friends via social networks on Shazam's own social Friends feed." (Mills)

WAITING IS A condition of being alive, a kind of simmering that allows desire and anticipation and fear and regret and imagination to steep as their maddening flavor profile matures. Waiting has been radically altered in contemporary life, its contours reimagined, the intervals between wanting and getting, losing and regaining, contracting very rapidly. I wonder if we're on the way to solving desire.

"FOR THE WHITNEY Biennial this year, Yukinori Yanagi, a Japanese-born conceptual artist, created two pieces with the help of some ants. For one, Mr. Yanagi assembled a replica of

Jasper Johns's *Three Flags* by pouring red, white, and blue sand into three Plexiglas boxes. Then he poured in live ants, inviting them to tunnel through the sand. As the ant farm got busy, the flag began to collapse." ("Animals Have Taken Over Art, and Art Wonders Why; Metaphors Run Wild, but Sometimes a Cow Is Just a Cow," *New York Times,* June 24, 2000)

WAIT AND SEE.

DUSK AT THE International Bar on First Avenue in Manhattan. I'm sitting at my favorite table, nearest to the front door, three feet from the well-stocked jukebox over which I have benevolent control this June late afternoon, Jonathan Richman, the Kinks, the Jam, *Beatles '65*, the Buzzcocks, and Chicago blues issuing into the bar that was characteristically so dark when I walked in that I instinctively put out my hands, my eyes adjusting soon to find the always-friendly, always-laughing Claire who served me a cold can of Schaefer (three bucks). I took it to the front table and watched the people traffic go by as songs slowly brightened the place, competing with the loud regulars up front who mistook my DeKalb Flying Corn T-shirt for the street in Brooklyn, for the street in the Bronx, *they're everywhere!*

But as usual I ducked the small talk to sit for a couple hours after an afternoon of work, to look out the window and to think and soak in the tunes and the three or so cans of beer I'll drink and love, leaving regretfully across the creaking wood floor after *Thanks!* and *See ya!*'s out into the dimming sunshine on the street which, after the hospitality and quiet, friendly dark of the soothing bar, feels warm and vibrant, somehow more welcome.

Before I'd left, someone had selected a doo-wop song on the jukebox, a tune I'd never heard before, and it played in the background as I scribbled something in my notebook—but the last minute or so snagged me in its splendor and floating grace, an ending so exquisite in its pretty changes, heart-in-the-throat cadences, and harmonies that I teared up. *God, who is this?* The song ended before I could dash over and look—there is no "last played" feature on this jukebox, and there was more than one doo-wop CD in the machine. I didn't catch enough of the song to even guess at a title, and it was too late to use my phone. I left the bar humming bare traces, the final moments of the song like excavated bones, already fading in the daylight. I went sifting and sifting, remembering and longing, all night.

DON'T YOU KNOW THAT IT'S SO?

*S*OMETIME BEFORE DAWN on February 11, 1963, Sylvia Plath opened the door of the oven in her flat at 23 Fitzroy Road in London and laid her head on a folded towel inside. She had already sealed the door to the bedroom where her two young children Nicholas and Frieda slept, after placing bread-and-butter sandwiches and glasses of milk by their beds. Plath's body was discovered by her nurse and the building's handyman at around 9 a.m. Roughly an hour later, she was pronounced dead by her physician, Dr. John Horder. Less than two miles away at 3 Abbey Road, the Beatles were thirty minutes into the daylong recording sessions that would result in their debut album, *Please Please Me*, released in the U.K. on March 22. At the moment when Dr. Horder declared Plath deceased, the Beatles were working on their first song of the day, "There's a Place."

> *. . . where I can go*
> *When I feel low, when I feel blue*
> *And it's my mind*
> *and there's no time when I'm alone*

I THINK ABOUT the confluence of death and birth on a gray February morning in London. Something—fandom? residue of a dream?—requires that I lay a kind of transparency of consequence over the two-mile grid of London streets and green Primrose Hill. Fantasy on my part, but look: Plath's home at two o'clock on the map, to Abbey Road's seven o'clock, sprawling Regents Park just south. What's revealed? Imagined links. Invisible correspondences. Plath's suicide and the Beatles' recording sessions overlapped, and in that alchemy I need to believe that something was forged, that a thick boundary was established, that the '50s ended and the '60s began—or if that's facile, that a rejection of the world gave way to a future erupting with possibilities. Or it's simply, indulgently, my own obsession for finding meaning where meaning doesn't exist, mania scored by a song.

It's impossible to know for sure how many young beat groups were toiling away in England on February 11, 1963. Among the soon-to-be-famous, the very young Rolling Stones (Bill Wyman and Charlie Watts had recently joined) were between gigs at Ealing Jazz Club on that date; the Who, not yet with the combustible Keith Moon, had played a grand total of six shows; Ray Davies was in art school; the Hollies were three months away from releasing their debut single; the Yardbirds weren't the Yardbirds, they were the Metropolitan Blues Quartet (and then, briefly, the Blue-Sounds); pop idol Cliff Richard had just released the movie *Summer Holiday*, another "Cliff Richard musical" on its way to out-grossing James Bond. On the day when Plath's body was removed from her apartment, the day that began her second life as a famous twentieth-century poet and tragic Wife of Hughes, no one knew that the Beatles' *Please Please Me* would become the presaging album that it would become, a brash step in a career that vitally affected popular music and our belief in its limits, possibilities, and promises. Plath's ending and the Beatles' beginning narrate a story that doesn't exist, and yet does.

> *In my mind there's no sorrow*
> *Don't you know that it's so?*
> *There'll be no sad tomorrow*
> *Don't you know that it's so?*

REALISM REQUIRES THAT characters move about in a world that looks like the world outside our windows, that they respond to conflicts that feel familiar, collide with other characters plausibly. One of the difficulties for the writers and actors on *Mad Men* was locating the correct pitch in communal events and individual responses. The show (sometimes clumsily) dramatized characters reacting to cultural events or trends in medias res, such as the widening generation gap (the Rolling Stones), the perceived escalation of random violence or machination unto peaceful idyll (Richard Speck, Charles Whitman, the IBM computer), the Vietnam War, recreational drug use, hippie communes, and integration in the workplace.[1]

What do we talk about as we talk about the present? Tethering dramatic exposition, historical context, and character development within period narrative art requires a careful hand. *Mad Men* writers were smart not to mention Speck by name in the "Mystery Date" episode in season five, as that might've imported the characters into an informed future when everyone knows Speck's name, infamy, and lurid place in pop culture. In the summer of '66, we weren't there yet. The writers acknowledged this again in that season's episode "Signal 30," when Don Draper corrects another character's misstating of Charles Whitman's last name; we weren't yet that familiar with his surname. That was a nice touch, as there's always more unfolding to come in life, more clarity and earned perspective on the horizon. I'm thinking also of "The Grown-Ups" episode in season three in which two characters squabble over something as Walter Cronkite's epochal coverage of President Kennedy's assassination plays out on a flickering television set in the background: the historic first unnoticed, then impossible to ignore. "A story really isn't any good," said Flannery O'Connor, "unless it successfully resists paraphrase, unless

---

1 And don't get me started on Don Draper dropping the needle on the first song of the second side of the Beatles' *Revolver* and hearing the portentous stirrings of John Lennon's "Tomorrow Never Knows," when he would've heard the cheerful optimistic march of Paul McCartney's "Good Day Sunshine." Lennon's apocalyptic stunner is the last song on *Revolver*.

it hangs on and expands in the mind." This is how memory works, too: a thing happens, and then a thing expands over time as it's sifted through memory. We're too close to events as they evolve to gauge their impact on us personally, let alone on culture at large.

Of course, people did talk in their rec rooms and bedrooms about Elvis's swiveling hips and the Dave Clark Five's long hair, about Woodstock, streaking, and disco, about Gen X, tramp stamps, and texting. How do we sound when we're reacting to what's right in front of us? Here's Vincent Kartheiser, who played *Mad Men*'s Pete Campbell, on public and personal histories as they played out in the series' fifth season: "The times are a-changing and in the first few episodes we've seen it make its way into Sterling Cooper Draper Pryce. Times have been changing for the last few years. There's been riots and integration and things have been changing but it hasn't affected the lives of these people as profoundly as maybe the history books would want you to believe." Kartheiser continues:

> Let's take something huge, like the war in Iraq. It's huge and in thirty years we'll look back and think that everybody's life was inundated with this war but for most of the people I know, including myself, it had very little effect on us. It has an effect, but we can't quite see it yet. It's the same with the 1960s, and we look back and say: "Oh, there were these great changes, everyone

must've felt it." It takes a while for these things to take effect in the exclusive upper- and middle-class office buildings. We're just starting to see it now. It's '66 and it's starting to hit home.

Around the same time, *Mad Men*'s creator Matthew Weiner discussed the show and the idea of history unfolding, also using the Iraq War as a touchstone. "The show is not a history lesson," he insists. "I don't want to ignore what's going on, but I always like to think about how we experience history. Very few times in your life do you wake up and find out that a plane has flown into the World Trade Center. The rest of it is very gradual and small. The war ended this year in Iraq. That will be marked in a history book, and someone, in the future, who is writing about this period, will write, 'In early 2012 the war was finally over and Obama went on to the election trail and blah-blah-blah,' but we didn't experience it that way. It was a blip, which was incredible because it was one of the longer wars that we've been involved in." He added, "You live your life. You want to eat, drink, be merry, maybe you will focus on your kid, maybe you will focus on your career, but the history part of it just becomes a mood."

Smaller dramas often take precedence as we move about; in hindsight we recognize the momentous cultural events that our daily grind overshadowed, the moods that crystallize as events. If we do realize that we may be inside a historic moment, we often react tentatively, as if gazing at puzzle pieces on the floor. I wonder what I did or said when I learned about that guy who blew up that building in Oklahoma before I knew Timothy McVeigh's now-unforgettable name. How did I react to the assassination attempt on Ronald Reagan in real time? To Kurt Cobain's suicide? I watched television, I stared at newspaper articles, I talked to people, I probably veered off-topic before too long, sidetracked by the pressing of my own life. If I were to write about those reactions, I'd resist having to characterize them as more dramatic and knowing than they actually were.

Over morning coffee a while back, my wife, Amy, and I talked idly about Facebook. If two actors play us thirty years from now, I wonder how their writers would dramatize our conversation, whether the characters would utter the name Mark Zuckerberg, the way Amy and I didn't, whether they'd make Large Pronouncements About Culture the way Amy and I didn't. We yawned and bungled our way through nascent reflection and the give-and-take of talking toward a decent, semithoughtful, hardly momentous conversation. Would our fictive stand-ins avoid our *Whatever*s and our *Well, you know what I mean*s? How will we talk about 2017 in 2047?

WE WERE FIGHTING. I don't remember many particulars. We weren't holding hands; I know that for sure. My then-girlfriend Janet was working at a trade bookstore in suburban

Washington D.C., and I drove in to see her, and on her fifteen-minute breaks we argued furtively but passionately outside on the front sidewalk. I remember a glass door slamming, wet eyes. We yelled at each other over the phone. One of those awful daylong arguments. What I know for certain is the date. May 25, 1986.

Our local spat backgrounded a day of national benevolence. Hands Across America was a benefit and publicity event organized by Ken Kragen, the man responsible for We Are the World. Inspired by an offhand comment from a fellow charity organizer, Kragen conjured hand-holding Americans creating a human chain stretching from the east to the west coast. Implemented by USA for Africa's founding executive director Marty Rogol, Hands Across America was certainly of its celebrity-charity era, but it ultimately raised $34 million to help elevate awareness and fight hunger and homelessness. What many scoffed at at the time, myself included, was the glaring divide between the event's ambition and its execution; hundreds of miles of the more inhospitable swaths of the country weren't covered by the chain, with many large cities trickily looping linked humans among multiple streets in order to account for enough miles. (Approximately 6.5 million people participated in the "chain" that ultimately covered 4,125 miles across seventeen states.) I remember David Letterman making withering jokes about managerial ineptitude and the miles-wide gaps. I remember snickering along.

Of course, there was also a commemorative song. "Hands Across America," written by Marc Blatte and John Carney, sung by session singers Joe Cerisano and Sandy Farina backed by Toto, was played concurrently on hundreds of radio stations at 3:00 p.m. EST that day, likely at the moment Janet and I were arguing during her snack break. I have no memory of hearing the song as it played, but I was aware of its existence, and was dismissive, as were many of my friends. (Our distance from sentiment was still lengthy following what we felt was the grandstanding during the "We Are the World" video the previous year. I hadn't cared to see Bruce Springsteen, Dionne Warwick, Billy Joel, et al. howling earnestly, however noble the cause.) The director of the official "Hands Across America" video was Bob Giraldi, who edited close-ups of large-eyed, weary-looking children and generic Americana imagery (farmlands, cityscapes, public parks) as ordinary folk and various celebrities (Kenny Rogers, Michael Douglas, Yoko Ono, and *Miami Vice*'s Don Johnson and Philip Michael Thomas among them) sang along to the song, clasped hands and raised them to blue skies through which eagles soared. Charged with scoring such loaded iconography, the track's synthesizers were set on Sincere.

The lyrics to "Hands Across America" are characteristic of charity-caroling, broad and sentimental, and provide irresistible subtext to my trivial, long-forgotten argument with my girlfriend. "I cannot stop thinking again and again," emotes

Cerisano, Michael Bolton's backup singer, "How the heart of a stranger / beats the same as a friend." *Learn to love each other*, the song commands. "See the man over there? He's my brother. / When he laughs I laugh. When he cries I cry. / When he needs me I'll be right there by his side." If "Hands Across America" played in the bookstore where Janet worked, we weren't listening, caught up as we were in our own melodrama of distance and pettiness.

The image of a squabbling couple against the background of Hands Across America seems terrifically ironic now, yet it occurred, a song playing somewhere as two people played out its opposite. Dave Alvin captures this dynamic beautifully in his song "4th of July"—recorded by X on their 1987 album *See How We Are*—in which a wearily arguing couple, jolted out of their solipsism by the noise of kids shooting fireworks, recognize that they're fighting on the nation's birthday, so blinded by spite and insularity that they failed to take note of communal celebrating happening literally outside their window. "Whatever happened, I apologize," the singer says to his girl. "So dry your tears and, baby, walk outside. It's the fourth of July." *We forgot!* he exclaims in disbelief as the song fades.

ONE OF THE many pleasures in writing about music is reading old issues of *Billboard* magazine. I've spent countless hours squinting at microfilm archives, nailing down a song's or an album's release date, industry buzz, chart appearance, chart disappearance. What I'm struck by each time I read is the way the past is recreated by Top 40, as if all along our adolescence was scored by pop songs.

An asphalt playground at a suburban Catholic grade school. September. As the Ramones sing, it's the end of the '70s. The songs charting on *Billboard*'s Top 100 this week embody character types: the kid who loves Charlie Daniels Band's "The Devil Went Down to Georgia" (#6), who excitedly talks about Skoal and fiddle playing and The South Will Rise Again to anyone who'll listen, secretly loves the Knack's "My Sharona" (#1) and can't admit it to his tobacco-chewing buddies; he thinks it's New Wave and cooler than he is and he plays the insistent drums and the dirty lyrics over and over in his head. That girl's parents like Barbra Streisand's new song "The Main Event/ Fight" (#3) and took in the movie last Friday on a "date night"; she'd rather forget about that, and that Ryan O'Neal looks a little like her dad, and so she plays ELO's "Don't Bring Me Down" (#5) downstairs in the basement over and over, dancing around with no one there. Pull wide, and the rest of the grade school playground comes into view, asphalt and grass fields dotted by darting kids, happy or forlorn, all moving to a soundtrack. The weird kids over by the tree, the ones who wear non-regulation skinny ties and put band buttons on their book bags, they're talking about Joe Jackson's "Is She Really Going Out with Him?" (#48), Sniff 'n' the Tears' "Driver's Seat" (#22), and Bram Tchaikovsky's "Girl of My Dreams" (#37), songs no one's heard of. Those two over there are sneaking cigarettes and laughing about Kiss's "I Was Made for Loving You" (#49), crowing to everyone within earshot that they knew the band was lame and a bunch of pussies in makeup. Within a couple of weeks, some of these kids will be dancing at parties to the Commodores' "Sail On" (#14) or Little River Band's "Lonesome Loser" (#12) or the Knack's "Good Girls Don't" (bubbling under at #82), fumbling among knees and bra straps, half-decoding lyrics, half-decoding each other's gestures; others will stay home in their bedrooms and listen dolefully as the radio plays Earth, Wind & Fire's "After the Love Has Gone" (#4) while the Friday Night Movie's on downstairs and Mom says, Why don't you come down and watch? Way out on the far edge of the school grounds, in the shadows, Dave Edmunds's "Girls Talk" (#86) or Nick Lowe's "Cruel to Be Kind" (#27) might be playing, but the words are complicated; some kids think they know what they mean, but they're probably getting them all wrong. M's "Pop Muzik" (#31) plays in the background some- where else, illuminating a place where even the cool kids won't go yet, someplace angular and futuristic that sounds like what high school might feel like.

Maybe a third of these songs will linger in memory; the rest will vanish. Yet lift the transparency of the Top 100 from this ordinary tableau of teenagers at recess, and something sticks to them that they absently rub at the rest of their lives: a hook in a chorus, a phrase that in a few words seemed to say everything

that they then couldn't, a chord change that when they're surprised by it decades later on the car radio or in the iCloud will
move them beyond words, beyond reason. They'll be unable
still to articulate what those songs are able to say, the stories
they tell just out of reach.

AROUND NOON ON January 28, 1986, I was happily cull-
ing records and 45s for my three-hour show on WMUC, the
University of Maryland campus radio station, when news broke
over the wire that the space shuttle Challenger had broken up
off the coast of Cape Canaveral, Florida, a little over a minute into its flight. Noisily, a student dashed into the newsroom,
which was adjacent to the DJ studio, and ran the story as it
unfolded. Like everyone there, I was listening intently. I'd forgotten that I'd already cued up my opening song. After the
brief headline and promises of updates, the student threw the
mike to me. I looked down in alarm at the turntable and poised
needle: raring to be unleashed was "Wreck-a-Party-Rock" by
King Kurt, an English psychobilly band prone to brawling and
onstage food fights. The song is wonderful nonsense, the sound
of drunken primates letting loose, all jungle rhythms and gut-
tural yelping, just the kind of pounding, beery weekend anthem
I prized. (I prize.) As the announcement of the shuttle tragedy
lingered in the charged air, with the news staff clamoring for
more information, I was faced with two options: play a wildly
inappropriate party song, or inflict dead air over the waves as

I scrambled to find and cue up a less trashy, somehow more-appropriate-for-the-moment song. I panicked, in my youth and amateurishness, and started the turntable.

I know: it's likely that I was the only person sensitive to my song choice, that the handful of listeners, half of whom were WMUC staff, weren't paying any attention. And yet this is how memory, song, and story conspire: I will eternally shame myself with this small incident, and two unrelated cultural moments—a graphic catastrophe, a silly song—will be forever entwined in my mind. "Wreck-a-Party-Rock" gained a new, irreverent video that day, and the awful, spiraling parts of the shuttle against a blue sky gained a soundtrack.

I WAS TRUSTING that some numerical data might refine—or more likely refute—my Sylvia Plath–Beatles equivalence theory. I got in touch with Yvonne Paul, First Point of Contact in Her Majesty's Passport Office at the General Register Office in the U.K., who helpfully provided me with some census information: in 1963, precisely 260,458 women died in England and Wales, of whom 82,090 were married, this according to "Table 15: Constructed analysis of 1963 deaths by age and marital condition" in The Registrar General's Statistical Review of England and Wales 1963 Part I. "Deaths at different ages by months of occurrence, January to December, 1963"—Table 16—narrows the data, documenting that 123 women between the ages of thirty and thirty-five died in the U.K. and Wales in

February, out of 31,145 total female deaths in the month. Some 31,741 men died in the U.K. and Wales in February. Numbers and columns.

Comings and goings. Plath was thirty when she died. Her death, one of 123, was statistically inconsequential, though eventually culturally significant. Sobering, wide-angle knowledge of the fatalities of an ordinary month in England should've dampened my desire to see in Plath's death and the Beatles' birth little more than coincidence; even describing the events as *intersecting* gives them more relation than they deserve. And yet I cling to narrative, to setting as metaphor. Squabbling with my girlfriend against the backdrop of Hands Across America is insignificant but for the context it provides me, the unintended illumination, decades later, of our self-absorption cast in sharp relief against larger suffering, and of earnest attempts to aid that suffering. Me? I stormed home that day, probably ignored the radio if it wasn't playing a song I liked, fumed in twenty-something vanity.

That day in '63, the Beatles played on. They ran through a dozen takes of "There's a Place" on February 11 before being satisfied, or anyway hurried along to the next song, "Seventeen" (soon to be retitled "I Saw Her Standing There"); they were up against the clock at EMI Studios and had nine more songs to complete before the sessions ended at precisely ten forty-five that night. Focused and energetic, they dashed through a con-densed version of their stage set under the watchful tutelage of producer George Martin, unaware that a writer named Sylvia Plath had died nearby, even less tuned to the gravitas I now give that death and its evocative proximity. Would Lennon, McCartney, Harrison, or Starr have even known who Plath was? (Lennon, maybe, though it's highly unlikely, even as well-read a twenty-two-year-old as he was. Plath's novel *The Bell Jar* was published under the pseudonym Victoria Lucas in the U.S. the month before her death; her first book of poems, *The Colossus*, came out in 1960 and several of the poems had appeared in U.K. literary journals, but her most famous and well-received book of poems, *Ariel*, wasn't published until 1965.) I don't know that Plath was a fan of the Beatles' music. At the time of her death, the band had released two singles in England, "Love Me Do" and "Please Please Me." The latter was the band's first big hit throughout the U.K., reaching the top spot on the *New Musical Express* and *Melody Maker* charts, but domination of the British Isles, let alone of North America, was still a year or so away. Who knows if Plath had heard "Please Please Me" on the radio while living in London, or, if she had, didn't feel at the age of thirty that the Beatles' strange-sounding music and girlish hair weren't hers to embrace.[2]

---

2 Ted Hughes: "In the U.K. the shock of the '60s is usually tied to the Beatles. But as far as poetry was concerned their influence was marginal, I think. The poetry shock that hit the U.K. in the '60s started before the Beatles. Sylvia responded to the first ripples of it. In a sense, *Ariel* is a response to those first signs, and she never heard the Beatles." (*Paris Review*, "The Art of Poetry," no. 71, Spring 1995) It's difficult to trust Hughes absolutely here, as he and Plath were estranged at the time of her death. They'd separated in September 1962; the Beatles' first single was released in October.

Either way, on the morning when Plath's lungs were overcome and her heart stopped, Lennon sang achingly on the lines "In my mind there's no sorrow" and "There'll be no sad tomorrow" and—against foolishness—I can hear in the words and melody an unintended, impossible threnody for a deeply despondent woman who retreated from the world. I also hear a song that heralds an unimaginable future. In *Revolution in the Head: The Beatles' Records and the Sixties*, Ian MacDonald describes "There's a Place" as a declaration of independence, "an assertion of self-sufficient defiance which, matched by music of pride and poignancy, marks a minor milestone in the emergence of the new youth culture."

Meanwhile, someone walking down Fitzroy Road or Abbey Road kept on walking, turned left, or right, and, distracted by his own ways of interpreting the causal world, went home to tea and papers.

JOURNEY TO THE MOON

THE SPACE AGE drifted all around me: Major Matt Mason toys in various heroic poses on the basement floor, plastic red-and-blue rockets ascending and landing, the interstellar playing out under the pool table as astral 45s by Eumir Deodato ("Also Spake Zarathustra 2001") and Vik Venus ("Moonflight") revolve on the family stereo. The latter was one of those novelty "cut-in" songs popular in the 1960s, a faux Q&A with astronauts using Top 40 song snippets as answers. New York's WMCA DJ Jack Spencer asked the questions. Samples:

Q: Commander Rah Rah, we'd like to ask you some questions now.

A: Goody goody gumdrops, my heart is doing flip-flops! [as warbled by 1910 Fruitgum Company]

Q: If you're confronted by any creatures as you explore the moon surface, what will you tell them?

A: Welcome me, love, I know you don't know me, take my hand, there's a lot you can show me! [Brooklyn Bridge]

Etc. It kept us kids in stitches. Also in high rotation in the rec room during the early and mid-1970s was *Journey to the Moon*, released in July of 1969 by Buddah Records in an attempt to celebrate and honor—and cash in on—the Apollo 11 moon-landing mission. Boasting on its cover "Recorded live on Earth, in Space, on the Moon," the album twined NASA command-control audio with bold narration and spacey acid-rock and psychedelic instrumentals. The music was recorded in Philadelphia with Sound of Genesis, a session group featuring then-unknown keyboardist Daryl Hall under the command of producer John Madara (best known for having cowritten "At the Hop" in 1957). Future singer-songwriter Tim Moore, also in the band, cowrote the bulk of the album with Madara, whose industry friend Len Barry of the Dovells fame ("You Can't Sit Down," "The Bristol Stomp") cowrote the title track. Under the auspices of Buddah Records' visionary president Neil Bogart, Madara and producer partner Tom Sellers created an album wholly of its prophetic, New Dawn era. Madara stated in an interview, "Neil Bogart wanted to be the first record company out with authentic conversations with the astronauts and others, including President Nixon, using original music that we composed," adding that *Journey to the Moon* "was approved by NASA, who sent in the tapes every day to us of the moon flight, which we used on the LP." The resulting album is trippy, corny, earnest, unintentionally funny, and wonderfully evocative.

How *Journey to the Moon* splashed down in our house in suburban Washington D.C., I'm not so certain. My dad probably picked up the album at Korvettes or Dart Drug. For decades he was employed as an engineer at IBM where, among other responsibilities, he worked with NASA on their unmanned scientific spacecraft program, as well as with navigation, meteorology, astronomical and earth-survey satellites, ballistic missile defense, telecommunication and highly classified military intelligence systems, launch-vehicle payload weight analysis and allocation, geosynchronous orbit and system reliability analysis, and Global Positioning Satellites. The back of the computer paper that he brought home from work for me to draw on spoke a language of ones and zeros that I never comprehended, but its futuristic cadence struck me; I grew up with lunar images decorating the house and plaques of commemoration and gratitude from NASA on the walls. *I Dream of Jeannie* on TV and Tang in the kitchen were for me both cultural and personal. While listening to *Journey to the Moon* in the rec room I'd unconsciously sift the hype and the myth of the Moon Landing era from the reality of my dad's job—of which, I must admit, I knew very little as a kid. ("He's an engineer," I'd tell kids on the playground, unsure if that meant that he rode around on a train all day.) But as I grew, I intuited that my dad had *something* to do with the moon landings. *Journey to the Moon* provided the score.

Beyond the autobiographical, the album matters as a pop touchstone for a lost era, a vinyl time capsule. The cover drawing of a full moon against a boundless-black background with sunlight dappling the surface in neon yellow-green—surely no color found in the natural world—announced the gravitas inside: this is an otherworldly record. Look: Music by Sound of Genesis. The song titles, set in a curve hugging the moon's lower half: "The Mystery of Space," "Sea of Tranquility," "Empty Void," "Nineteen Ninety-nine," and . . . "Space Rock"? Well, it was the late '60s. Amps were bigger, hair was longer, festivals were sprouting, moods were altering, the universe was infinite. Why not rock out and celebrate space?

Nothing less than a heroic *Monday Night Football*-type theme for space geeks, "Journey to the Moon" kicks off the album with a lonely horn offering two notes a fifth apart while an announcer, his voice tinny and far-away, gravely intones the opening passage from the Book of Genesis. Heady stuff. A honky-tonk piano tumbles in, the band catches up, and the interstellar groove is on. Imagine if in 1972 Edgar Winter snorted a few lines and impulsively recorded a faster version of his stomping "Frankenstein"; then imagine a blend of the Telstars, Davie Allan and the Arrows, and some nameless sub-urban garage band lumbering hopefully through a prog-rock instrumental (while hoping no one's listening), and you'll get an idea of the vibe in the title track.

The song ascends via calls-and-responses between racks of keyboards and fat horns, lashed on by tambourines and bon-gos, leading to the bridge's wandering bars of cosmological organ meant to evoke the infinite winding miles into dark space aboard the cruising Apollo spacecraft. Things slow down in the final third as the band recedes while a *boing boing* synthesizer effect gives way to the return of the disembodied Voice who reminds us, as if we haven't been dabbing our eyes as we've been dancing, that man "now has the audacity to reach for the stars, and get there." Corny, yes, but this monumental echo of John F. Kennedy's Space Race mandate sends the song soaring to its anthemic finish and anoints the project with the kind of late-1960s American pride and exceptionalism that really must've sounded, and felt, like the theme for the epoch. So commercially promising was its exhilarating blend of celebratory groove and boundless optimism that "Journey to the Moon" was released as a single by Buddah. But the wake imposed by, among others, the 5th Dimension's monster hit "Aquarius/Let the Sunshine In," trippily similar in vibe and ethos, kept the 45 off of the *Billboard* charts.

In the album's liner notes, Richard Robinson writes, "Despite the highly scientific reality of the Apollo project, fantasy is still an inherent part of the journey. We don't know exactly why we're going, the moon is there so we have to go. And we certainly don't know where this display of a million years of discovery and sophistication will lead mankind." Madara, Sellers, and Moore were charged with scoring these august sentiments, and the fantastical moon landing, the experimental climate in the country, and the rise of FM progressive rock demanded this curious, now-dated artifact of evocative generic rock. The phrase "evocative generic rock" seems paradoxical, but *Journey to the Moon* evokes the NASA zeitgeist at the dawn of the 1970s, an idealistic marriage of crew-cut ingenuity and long-haired psychedelia, outer and inner space commingling.

As a kid rocking out in the rec room, I didn't register any of this, of course; I just dug the album's playfulness. Buddah took out a full-page advertisement for *Journey to the Moon* in *Billboard* on August 2, 1969, crowing, "THE 30 BILLION DOLLAR ALBUM," surely a reference to the Apollo-mission price tag, not the album's recording budget. The production values strike these twenty-first-century ears as old-fashioned, and that's part of the fun. Throughout, Victor Jay's narration is buttoned-up, Cronkite Serious, lending an air of legitimacy to the enterprise. Sound of Genesis creates the "modern" ambience behind the NASA and astronaut chatter: the analog music bouncing off of the glimmering Pacific, cheerful and triumphant.

If naive in retrospect, it's also movingly redolent of the era. In *Dark Side of the Moon: The Magnificent Madness of the American Lunar Quest*, Gerard Degroot essays the moon landing with a long view, wondering if the event lacked lasting significance. "People accepted that that one small step was a giant leap for mankind simply because Armstrong said it was so," Degroot argues. "Few paused to consider how walking around the moon in a space suit brought progress to mankind." He asks how the mission helped the starving in Africa, or the plight of Vietnamese peasants mired between communism and capitalism. He adds, "Did African-Americans watching the landing in a fetid shack in Alabama suddenly shout: 'Golly, my life is so much better because Neil took that small step!' Some people obviously thought so." *Journey to the Moon* steers clear of such arguments, dazzled by achievement, celebrating it in song, assuming the cultural importance of a sun-splashed spectacle. Certainly Buddah Records had consumerism in mind; the same year that the label released this album they released *The Amazing Mets*, celebrating the New York Mets' improbable season. Both albums had a stake in their own commercial success; both originated, in part, in exploitation. But decades down the line, *Journey to the Moon* feels less exploitative than simply, innocently, awestruck.

IF INTEGRAL CALCULUS has a nerd-heroic theme song, it's "The Computer," Madara's variety-show song-painting conjuring festive images of NASA's computer feats against an infinite dark and the receding earth. The imaginatively titled "Space Rock" caps off the first side with forced cheer, generic go-go music trying a bit too hard to project rockin' astronauts; I can't picture Neil or Collins or Buzz frugin' on the surface of the moon, as much as I try. "A Walk on the Moon" is more appropriate musically—despite the touch of what sounds like a banjo filtered through a lunar module flight board—a loping, easy stroll of a song with bright, optimistic chord changes. Prefaced by a brief, mysterious sitar/keyboard/guitar piece (the conclusion of "Empty Void"), "Nineteen Ninety-nine" doesn't offer the abstract futuristic tones of the unknown you might expect from the title; instead, a chirpy flute-and-horn melody sits atop an arrangement that skips along, suggesting an upbeat tomorrow. Three decades away at the album's release, the year 1999 must've felt close in spirit, however idealized the cultural projection turned out to be.

Winding among the instrumentals and balancing out the album are Jay's straightforward narration of the Apollo flight chronology, and segments, ranging from four to eight minutes, of *audio vérité*: NASA speaking with the astronauts from their liftoff to their minutes on the moon's surface to their reentry in the atmosphere; President Nixon's famous phone call to the astronauts; and, of course, Armstrong's immortal words upon stepping onto the moon. The album concludes atmospherically, with several seconds of studio-created lunar wind as Jay sums up the significance of the events between July 16 and 24. At just under thirty-four minutes, *Journey to the Moon* manages to document, teach, and groove at the same time. If not an engineering feat rivaling NASA's, it's a pretty impressive bundling together of disparate parts.

TWO YEARS AFTER the release of *Journey to the Moon*, an article appeared in *Billboard* announcing that Buddah Records was expanding into education programs. Select Buddah artists were to supply "background music for scientific, social studies, art, literature, and geography lessons put together by Planetariums Unlimited for classroom instruction." None other than *Journey to the Moon*'s Victor Jay was employed, in conjunction with classroom celebrations of the recent moon landings. Alas, I don't recall Sister Irene in the All-Purpose Room at St. Andrew the Apostle School dropping the needle on *Journey to the Moon*. Perhaps with this educational "tie-in" initiative, Buddah was trying to distance itself from its bubblegum-pop heritage; I don't know how successful or not was the move. *Journey to the Moon* did not fare terribly well commercially and remains out of print. That's criminal. But its eBay and Discogs prices are reasonable, and online you can find plenty of bemused commentary about the album and the odd downloadable song. Until *Journey to the Moon* is re-released, those of us lucky enough to have grown up with the album in the 1970s will content ourselves with memories of a curio, in its way both a crass and a loving accolade to the Space Race, psychedelic rock, and our once star-bright future.

IN THE MORNING I'LL RISE ABOVE

*I*N 1928, THE Victor Talking Machine label in Memphis, Tennessee, released a ten-inch shellac recording by Ishmon Bracey, a twenty-seven-year-old blues singer-guitarist from the Mississippi Delta. He'd been worried about the goings-on of his women, and his story arrives as many great narratives do, in expressionistic shards: Bracey's got his regular woman, and his "sometime" woman, too, who has a kid but who comes running to Bracey at night. Both women steal from him. He warns his sometime woman that his regular gal will cut her, or maybe shoot her, if she finds her, that she's the meanest woman he's ever seen. When he asked her politely for water one day, she gave him gasoline. "I got four, five puppies, got one shaggy hound, it takes all them dogs to run my women down," Bracey laments. Oddly, in the midst of singing about his troubles Bracey drops in a one-verse infomercial for Palmer's Skin Success, a popular cream used for lightening skin complexion. ("If you want your women to look like the rest.") It's hard to know whether Bracey sings with scorn and disgust or out of sympathy and with a wink, warbling nasally behind sincerity and guardedness in a studio somewhere in Memphis. After a suggestion by the Mississippi talent broker H. C. Speir, Bracey conceived of his song as a blues for a Saturday. Was there something beyond Speir's commercial instincts that suggested christening this song after a cheerless Saturday? Was there something in the song's subject, in the lead-up to cutting loose that inspired Bracey? Maybe he's hungover. Maybe his sometime woman causes trouble mostly on the weekends. Maybe Speir intuited that the singer feels the tug of Sunday's salvations, taking stock of the sorry and the profane with his guitar in hand.

Bracey wrote songs and performed for several more years, working alongside some of the great Delta musicians, and then drifted away from the blues. Following a decades-old calling, he became an ordained minister in 1951 and stopped singing secular music altogether, preferring to testify in the Mississippi Baptist churches of his upbringing. "Thank God I have changed," he reportedly told friends. "Saturday Blues" redeemed.

Somewhere else in the Volunteer State, later that night, Red Foley and his Cumberland Valley Boys are carousing in the deep, dark, and wild woods. "Tennessee Saturday Night," originally issued in 1948 on the Decca label as the B-side of a ten-inch shellac, is a good-time swing ballad extolling the fun to be had when the moon goes up and inhibitions come down. Bowing to mid-century convention, songwriter Billy Hughes throws muted light on the frolicking, carefully veiling nudity in the shadows of decorum. The lure of a weekend's peak, the evening devoted to dancing and drinking and letting go, is translated by Hughes into code for boozing and fucking, time-honored lyrical camouflage. Couples are in the woods "looking for romance," but the moon's "a little bashful and it seldom shines," so what happens in the dark stays there. The tension in Hughes's lyrics arrives in the shimmy of "civilized people . . . going native on a Saturday night," tensions made all the more palpable by Foley and the Valley Boys' sprightly arrangement and performance, the fiddles and pedal steel guitars yearning for the tops of the pine trees. At this nameless joint, hidden "where the tall corn grows," men and women "get their licks from an old fruit jar" (predating Carl Perkins's line in "Blue Suede Shoes") and dance in the dark, the helpful bartender having taken out the lights with his boot.

What a blast! But there's danger in the air—someone on the dark floor's got a gun, and everyone "acts just right, 'cause it's gonna be a funeral if you start a fight." In Hughes's terms, folks "struggle and they shuffle" until the sun comes up, delicate diction for a Saturday night of screwing and fighting. "Tennessee Saturday Night" hit number one on March 19, 1949, and remained on the *Billboard* country charts for nearly three months.

"Gonna push the clouds away, let the music have its way, let it steal my heart away, and you know I'm goin'." On Saturday nights, the journey is as jubilant as the destination. So affirms

John Fogerty in "Almost Saturday Night" from his self-titled album, released on Asylum in September of 1975. This narrative's fractured, too: there's a train bringing the rodeo to town, or is it bringing the singer home? A radio's playing outside the window (a bedroom? a train compartment?), but it competes with the bells at the train crossing, or from an imagined Gibson in the hands of a Chuck Berry wannabe. The story is embodied in the singing, exultant melody, and arrangement that praise and make passionate contact with the expectations of a long-awaited weekend night. Six years after Fogerty released the song, Welshman Dave Edmunds issued his own rollicking version (on his album *Twangin'*), its joy elevating the song's hopes and promises into a universal, trans-oceanic desire: *bye-bye tomorrow*. The most powerful word in the song is *almost*. The taste of a Saturday night's recklessness and exhilaration is more rousing at the brink of maybe, when anticipated, when prayed for.

I FELT BOUND and placeless, the kind of in-between granted by an epic Appalachian thunderstorm. I was heading west on Route 50, somewhere between Clarksburg and Parkersburg, West Virginia. Or was it Parkersburg and Athens, Ohio? Anyway, the wipers were going like mad. The constants: torrential, horizontal rain and the urging of Joe Boyd, an evangelical minister on WVGV gospel radio, 89.7 FM, broadcast out of tiny West Union, West Virginia. I'd tuned in after I'd grown bored with my iPod, on the search for some hills-and-holler color. The station promised "Old-fashioned, KJV, Gospel Preaching," and Boyd's voice cut through the lightning static as the road slipped perilously in and out of focus. I slowed down as Boyd's sermon grew in intensity, crackling through the speakers, warning of impending doom, and lamenting in fiery tones the duped sinner who believes against the righteousness of Jesus and his Word and the self-erasing hosanna acceptance of that Word into your heart. Boyd extemporized from his audio pulpit, his voice booming through the car as the sky darkened and low lightning lit up the near space above my sorry head. The rain fell in sheets.

OVERHEARD:

Every time you move like that, I gotta go to Sunday mass . . .

. . . You can't go to church, child, and sing all day Sunday, and then go out and get drunk and greet the devil on a Monday.

SATURDAY NIGHT BRINGS both pledges and lies of limitlessness, of a night never ending, a jukebox always playing, dance partners always spinning, car wheels revolving on roads that never end in daylight. But no matter how it's beerily dismissed, or blithely ignored in the clutch-and-heave of Saturday-night lovemaking, Sunday always comes.

Here's a triptych, the soundtrack for the first panel provided by that old survivor Jerry Lee Lewis, feeling his way through

Kris Kristofferson's devastating "Sunday Morning Coming Down," a performance from *Mean Old Man*, released in 2010. There are no guest stars here, no manufactured, dual-studio stunt-duets on this performance: all we've got is The Killer at the mike, with tasteful and unobtrusive country accompaniment. The giddy steel guitars that landed in the treetops in "Tennessee Saturday Night" now lay down reproachful, sobbing notes. There's nary a piano in earshot, so Lewis can't hide behind his bravura playing and distracting, stool-kicking showiness. The vocals are weathered and lived-in, regretful and sighing, offered by a man in his mid-seventies who's seen more than his share of repudiating Sunday mornings. Producer Jim Keltner was initially concerned that the song might not fit Lewis well. And then Lewis started singing. "When we got to the point where we were actually recording, I could feel it all throughout my bones," Keltner told National Public Radio. "He just takes you right there, tells you exactly what this guy is thinking and where he is. It's just amazing how he made that song his own."

He wakes, his head pounding, and reaches for a restorative beer, joking to himself that he'll have one for dessert, too. Putting on his "cleanest dirty shirt," he heads outside to a world moving on its own accord, insensible to the agonies inside of him. A kid kicks and cusses at a can; someone's frying chicken; a girl laughs as her dad pushes her on a swing. A communally sung hymn issues from a nearby Sunday school, and the man stops to listen before he trudges back home. The music and the voices and the praising melt with a far-off bell ringing, repeating "through the canyons like the disappearing dreams of yesterday." Kristofferson wrote the song early in his career, and it became a big hit for Ray Stevens in 1969 and for Johnny Cash in 1970 (the year Kristofferson released his own version on his debut album). Down the decades it's been recognized as among the bleakest and most brutal reckonings, with the scolding brightness of a Sunday morning, a bottoming-out spiritual admission of loss "somewhere along the way."

Jerry Lee Lewis, who's spent his career and personal life with only occasional truces between his sacred and secular hostilities, sings "Sunday Morning Coming Down" as if the song's complications and bitter candor are as essential to him as his pulse. They probably are. Lewis has fought decades-long addictions to alcohol and drugs, to fame and sex, all the while unable to banish the cautionary voices from the Pentecostal churches of his youth in Ferriday, Louisiana. In the early 1970s he released a gospel album (*In Loving Memories*), recorded spirituals at a church in Memphis, and for a while earnestly swore off honky-tonk and rock-and-roll performances; the redemption didn't take, the footlights and late nights and booze and women too tempting, too much his to covet and own. In "Sunday Morning Coming Down" Lewis becomes an interpreter for anyone wishing he were stoned to blur the truths of a blank Sunday morning, who feels alone, who admits that "there's nothing short of dying, half as lonesome as the sound / On the sleeping city sidewalks, Sunday morning coming down." Listening, one frankly wonders how much time Lewis has left, and whether a reckoning of mortality brought this uncompromising song to his lungs.

Center panel, later that day. A man sits alone in Room 16 in a lousy motel somewhere on the edge of the lousy part of town. He's been holed up there for three weeks, resisting calling his ex on the payphone only to hear her hang up on him again. He thinks maybe he'll take a drive on this Sunday afternoon, out into the hills or across the parched farmlands, or down to the river for the breeze, but he'll probably stay just where he is, because "this small room, it seems to understand." If the song describes a paralyzed man, the performance is dynamic and muscular. The Blasters' "Just Another Sunday" (written by Blaster songwriter Dave Alvin with John Doe of X) appears on the band's 1985 *Hard Line* album. The arrangement mimics the ebb and flow of the singer's frustrations: ruminative verses lamenting his sorry state heave into the chorus where the band stops noodling around and commits to a driving ensemble performance—all growling guitars and eighth notes—fueled by bitterness and the desire to fight through to the other side of it.

As is the case with virtually all Blasters songs from this fertile period of their career, before sibling dissention and industry factors derailed the band, singer Phil Alvin—he of the peerless, ageless rock-and-roll voice—commits to his brother's words with Biblical vehemence. On this ordinary Sunday, preachers "got their heavens to sell" while he's stuck in a seedy motel room, its fluorescent reproach a poignant substitute for the church's vertical splendors and communal worshipping, for natural light filtered through pretty stained glass. Last night seems far away now—maybe he drank at a bar or alone in his room watching television's promises sold by corny, come-on commercials and music videos. The preachers can have their heaven and hell. Hindered and sulky, he'll stay where he is.

Third panel, later that evening. A couple's arguing in their kitchen, battling their way to some kind of truce. This is the first day of the rest of their lives, he insists to her, and there's no pretending that everything's okay. The tableau is lousy: he's a self-described bloodshot deadbeat, and her mascara's bleeding tears down her face. They're a young couple facing the fact that ecstatic Saturdays turn to hopeful Sundays turn to remorseful Mondays. As Green Day's "Church on Sunday" races to its anthemic chorus, the couple lurches toward a compromise: "If I promise to go to church on Sunday," he says, "will you go with me on Friday night?" It's a simple question, and the melody makes it hopeful, ascending on the phrase "Friday *night*." But the question is burdened by a vexed past—lies, likely, and mistrust, and disappointments as shared desires and visions pull apart.

Characteristically hook-driven and enthusiastically played, the tune appears on *Warning* (2000), a relatively unheralded Green Day album resting between the band's early successes

(*Dookie, Nimrod,* "Good Riddance [Time of Your Life]") and their worldwide *Billboard*-and-arenas dominance (*American Idiot* and its Tony Award–nominated Broadway adaptation). The autobiographical "Church on Sunday" is arguably the first fully adult song that Billie Joe Armstrong and the band produced, an honest rock-and-roll struggle between the excesses of snotty punk nihilism and a mature life devoted to faith and community. The tension in the middle has this young couple in its grip: if I do what you want, will you do what I want? Can we balance this weekend so that it doesn't topple into hangovers and recrimination? Can this work? He assures her that he'll earn her respect, but the eternal present tense of the song's resolution offers little closure. Next weekend's still a long way off.

TENSIONS BETWEEN SATURDAY night's excesses and Sunday morning's sober inventories are sometimes too graphic to resolve. In 1950, Columbia Records issued a 78-rpm single by Ted Daffan's Texans, "I've Got Five Dollars and It's Saturday Night," a lively ode to cash and liberty (and wine, women, and song). Armed with five dollars—the equivalent of maybe fifty bucks today—the singer's ready to shrug off the hard week behind him and head to the bar. The Texans swing effortlessly behind Daffan's crooning, the lilting horns and plucked guitar solo translating the singer's relaxed pleasure. "It's gonna go on till way past one," Daffan gushes, fingering the change in his pockets, "Gonna have fun tonight, gonna get right tonight." The promise? "Everything will be all right 'cause tonight is Saturday night."

A year later, Daffan's song would be reborn. Songwriter and guitarist Webb Pierce, a popular presence on the *Louisiana Hayride* radio show, had released a number of successful country singles in and around Louisiana, his home state. In the early 1950s Pierce was between moving from the California-based 4 Star label to the larger Decca label, and he took this freeing opportunity to interpret Daffan's hit song. For obscure reasons, Pierce transformed Daffan's celebration of Saturday night into a spiritual testimonial. (According to country-music historian Colin Escott, Pierce claimed at the time that the melody was in the public domain and so free for Pierce to do with it what he wished, but allegedly Pierce knew that the melody was Daffan's, and thus was careful to give Daffan cowriting credit.) Released as a B-side on Pierce's own Pacemaker label in 1951 and credited to Webb Pierce and His Southern Valley Boys, "I Got Religion on a Saturday Night" is essentially Daffan's, with redemptive lyrics provided by Pierce. The song's performed in the same key but the arrangement is more sprightly, and Pierce sings as if his urgency to testify trumps Daffan's to whoop it up. Here too the singer has been worn down by the workweek but looks forward to going to church "where the folks live right" because "religion is my might, tonight." Willfully ignoring the place where the lights are bright ("'cause music and dancing, that ain't right"), Pierce dismisses dance halls and taverns as heathen joints.

What precisely happened on a mid-century Saturday night that got Pierce his religion is left unsaid, his conversion implied in the song's swinging, upbeat credence of a life devoted to God and church, of the deliverance of five dollars to the collection plate, not to a tavern's till. Virtually anti-songs of each other, Daffan's and Pierce's takes on Saturday night embody the conflict inherent in pleasure and repentance, an enduring, eternal dance scored by fiddle, steel guitar, and upright bass. Paradoxically, within a few years Pierce would write one of the eternal honky-tonk odes to barroom drinking, "There Stands the Glass" (covered by Jerry Lee Lewis, among many others). That song's essaying of alcoholism and tavern romance is so vivid that upon its release it was banned by some Southern radio stations.

AFTER TWENTY OR so minutes, the landscape affected by Joe Boyd's rising-and-ebbing preaching was nearly too much to bear. I considered pulling over and . . . not testifying, or saying *Yes,* so much as surrendering. I was scared, and I didn't know if I was spooked by the novelty of a fiery evangelical sermon roaring from my car speakers or by that sermon's meanings and its vivid intentions for me. The not-entirely-welcome surprise of a homily. A couple of times I considered turning off the radio, but, rationalizing my desire to hear some local color before that color evaporated, I instead tuned in. I listened. Sun broke through at last, and as Route 50 ascended from the valley through which Boyd's voice resounded, the rain lessened. I gradually left that mystery behind, though I was tattooed.

This was late morning, on a Sunday. I'd been driving for a couple of hours after two days and nights of hard drinking with my buddies in a cabin in the hills of Great Cacapon, West Virginia. All weekend, Bracey's and Foley's and Fogerty's and The Killer's and the Blasters' and Green Day's and Daffan's and Webb's songs, and hundreds of others, boomed from the deck speakers down into the darkening hills and hardscrabble pitch pine and hickory trees leading to the quiet Cacapon River, as we drank cases of beer and talked and laughed and grilled meats and head-banged and air-guitared until the early morning hours.

Now, on Route 50, emerging from the ominous dark of a summer thunderstorm and of my own misgivings about pleasures and excesses, I was exhausted and hungover, my defenses perilously low. I'd driven from mindless fun (there'd been drunken stumbles at the cabin, some low-rent fireworks, a busted window) into the valley of a proselytizing sermon. Were I a character in a short story, you could say that I was ripe for an epiphany, as I was helplessly enthralled and shamed by, and yet stubbornly resistant to, the blazing homilies issuing from WVGV, a sermon cried by a fervent, faceless voice that was as sure to disappear from signal range as quickly as it had crackled to life.

IN SAN FRANCISCO, Ty Segall is working through his own dilemma, his amplifiers cranked. He's hoping that some distortion will help clear the air. He's singing "Thank God for Sinners," a raw, fraught anthem from his 2012 album *Twins*. He's out on the street, he's looking for her—she gives him sweets and he's not done with her yet. In the tradition of offering gratitude for those who elevate us, who provide purpose and ballast, Segall's perversely thanking God for sin and sinners and for the love they give to him. "In the morning," he assures himself, "I'll rise above." The song's really loud, murky, and heavy, mid-paced, as if Segall—a one-man band—is playing in a kind of sonic mud. It's hard to tell if it's being played in the late, late hours of a Saturday-night overindulgence, or in the early hours of Sunday's comedown; the song's pitched somewhere between hangover and healing. Sinning is elevating Segall, nourishing him, yet halfway through the song, he begs: "Won't you please just stop, so I can make it through?" Something during the night provides him with just enough, and whatever it is, he's grateful for the way it triumphs over him, for its dangerous appeal and temporary fuel.

Poor Bob Venable. He's so tangled in sin and deliverance that he's made of it a permanent knot. The Texan songwriter and guitarist wrote "When Sin Stops" in 1958 for his band the Nighthawks to record and issue as a regional single. I came across this relatively unknown song via the *Nasty Rockabilly* series—a terrific German-label multi-volume compilation of obscure, one-off 1950s and '60s singles—and it has an interesting history. The Nighthawks' recording was produced in a

New Mexico studio by Norman Petty, Buddy Holly's producer; Holly's backup singers contributed to the Nighthawks' song and alerted Holly that "When Sin Stops" might be in his wheelhouse. After the Nighthawks' released their single on the Hamilton label, Holly recorded the song for an unknown Lubbock, Texas, radio DJ and performer named Waylon Jennings. It was Jennings's first single (released on the Brunswick label in 1959) and an initial link in the chain of tragic associations between him and Holly.

Holly's influence is palpable on the Nighthawks' version, chiefly in guitarist Eddie Reeves's hiccupping lead vocal and in the song's ingenuous, sock-hop rockabilly groove. Of greater interest is the song's wrestling with sin and love, made painfully blatant in the singer's efforts to compartmentalize his girl's obvious lascivious charms away from whatever respectful and proper love they might (they must?) share. Gamely, Reeves sings one of the more brutal lines in American rock and roll: "When sin stops, love begins." As if the equation were ever that simple. She walks through the door and his temperature soars; she fibs and rolls her eyes, but he begs her to not stop (and the backing singers also implore her to go on). He knows it's not right, that the sinning has to stop before he can love her, but her lips are all he sees, and that's a problem that even the most innocuous, featherweight melody can't forgive, or erase. I like to think that, like Segall in "Thank God for Sinners," the Nighthawks perform "When Sin Stops" at a kind of threshold, one night's romps leaving traces of regrets that the next day's reckonings dress up as pieties, or as hard-won truths, or as salvation, depending. When sin and love meet, we're at a blurred edge, between Saturday's nodding off and Sunday's stirring.

BAFFLEMENT, CLARITY, AND MALICE

"**I** DON'T THINK THAT'S a particularly good line. I think it's a lousy one, actually. I prefer the line before it, 'With these vulgar fractions of the treble clef.' That's just my personal preference. The other one's a bit of an untidy payoff, one of the worst lines on the record."

"Seriously? I love it! It's a line I'd use in a pub."

"Well, yeah. I suppose you're right. . . ."

THIS EXCHANGE BETWEEN Elvis Costello and journalist Timothy White appears in *Musician* magazine from October of 1983. The line Costello's dismissing with characteristic insolence is "I wish you luck with a capital *F*," from his song "Love Went Mad" on *Punch the Clock*. Like White, I loved the line, thought it was hilarious and spiky. I couldn't imagine actually saying it, but I could imagine overhearing it, envious of the one who was so clever. That Costello liked his preceding line better disappointed me. At the time I was wrestling with Costello's lyrics, moving as so many of his admirers do between cherishing his most incisive, cutting observations and wrinkling my brow at his willfully obscure lines. "Vulgar fractions of the treble clef." *Huh?* Wishing someone luck with a *Fuck you*, now *that* I got.

I wanted Costello to sing to me clearly about the heart, about teenage swooning and naked embarrassment. For a while I'd been wrestling with "Man Out of Time" from his previous album, *Imperial Bedroom*, a song I now link with a deep and disarming crush I had when I was sixteen. From a well-worn storyboard: she worked on the newspaper at her high school, the all-girl sister institution to the all-boy Catholic school I attended. We'd meet after school at a print shop in an industrial area in Silver Spring to work on layout, debate pica width, the sizes and quality of grainy black-and-white photos. She had red hair that fell casually and a vibrant, throaty laugh. Later in the spring, we were both among the editors selected to attend a journalism convention at Columbia University in New York City. We had adjoining rooms in a hotel, hung out in sweatpants and sweatshirts; there was 3 a.m. flirting, and sprawling, noisy Manhattan outside of our windows, the vast city echoing the enormity of my feelings for her and the din of my own inadequacies. The end of the semester meant the end of the time we'd spend together. I'd called her, we'd talked, but I hadn't made a move, too shy and uncertain and, frankly, baffled in the face of my own feelings. ("Let's have some new clichés," Samuel Goldwyn commanded.) The newness and urgency of that early crush are stoked every time I listen to "Man Out of Time." Though the lyrics continue to stiff-arm me, the mid-paced melody's grandeur and glorious, sorrowful changes narrate those dumbstruck days of confusion and all kinds of romantic doubt.

Costello himself was facing serious misgivings in the early 1980s. Lingering were the bruises left by his reckless 1979 confrontation with Stephen Stills and Bonnie Bramlett in a Holiday Inn bar in Columbus, Ohio. The controversy of the fatuous remarks he made that night would follow him for years, despite numerous public apologies and sober regrets. His fame was infamous, and his songs were graphically evoking life, both at home and in hotels, marked by strife, cruelty, and drunken misbehavior. By the time he was writing the batch of songs for *Imperial Bedroom*, he was questioning his very identity. He's since described "Man Out of Time," a song that originated in profound despair, as the key song on that album. As he put it several years after the song's release: "A picture of decay, corruption, and betrayal. At the time it all seemed to suit rather well." Later, he clarified the unhappy picture:

> It was being an "adult" that was most of the problem.
> That and the fact that there seemed to be little time for
> "sober reflection." The public and private upheavals
> of the previous four or five years had heightened my
> already-melancholy disposition.

I intend that most "private" matters should remain that way but when the opening track is called "Beyond Belief" and the key song of a record is entitled "Man Out of Time," you don't have to be a detective or a psychiatrist to work out what is going on.

Disgusted, disenchanted, and occasionally in love, "Man Out of Time" was the product of a troubling dialogue with myself that continued through my more-regretful moments.

COSTELLO RECALLS LOOKING at his reflection in the window of a Scandinavian tour bus in the dead of winter—this was probably in early 1981—"without any idea who the hell I was supposed to be. I was trying to think or feel my way out of a defeated and exhausted frame of mind to something more glorious."

This was resolved in song, one shivering, hungover morning in manicured gardens of a remote Scottish hotel. The house in which we were staying had played a very minor part in one of Britain's most notorious political scandals, apparently serving briefly as a bolt-hole for one of the disgraced protagonists. I actually delighted at the thought of this sordid history; it suited my mood. I can't say that the words and ideas that emerged from these experiences were exactly welcome news to some of the band members. Like I could give a damn.[3]

ALONE, COSTELLO DEMOED "Man Out of Time" at Pathway Studios in London in August of 1981. At this point he's singing the song without really believing in it—or so it sounds, with the basic four-on-the-floor beat and kiddie Farfisa organ. Most demos are hesitant by nature, and Costello hasn't returned to the song's origin yet, changed; he's somewhere between inspiration and effect. Three months later at George Martin's AIR Studios, he recorded two versions of the song with the Attractions, one a messy, noisy affair that found the band thrashing away tunelessly, Costello howling like a B-movie maniac, the musicians afraid or otherwise unwilling to face the song's noxious beauty. "We were trying to beat the songs into submission," Costello confessed.

They eventually worked out the elegantly sprawling arrangement that appears on *Imperial Bedroom*. The transformation from the band's first attempt—snippets of which are included as the intro and outro of the album version—to the final result is striking. Rather than thrash the truth out of the song, the band members—Costello on guitar, Steve

---

3 Within a few years, Costello would break up his band the Attractions. (For the first time.)

Nieve on piano and organ, Bruce Thomas on bass, and Pete Thomas on drums—carefully but powerfully evoke a sense of gaudy shame, Nieve's twinkling grand piano offering an ironic and witty commentary on the fall-from-grace trope. They've slowed things down, the song needing a measured pace for the reckoning the sorry singer makes of himself and others. Played in stately 4/4 time, the song consists of three extended twenty-one-bar verses, a five-bar bridge, and a six-bar chorus. (A middle section, if as emotionally weighty as the rest, would've brought the whole thing down.) And somewhere during the sessions Costello found his melody, or it discovered him, in the achingly pretty lines he phrases as musical equivalents of rue-ful headshaking. As the band subdues things in the last verse, Costello drapes phrases onto the changes, sometimes pushing against the beat, sometimes surrendering, sometimes moving in between, following the movement between heart and head. He sings the words in ways that enact their deep and private meaning.

For himself. For me, and for many other listeners, the lyr-ics were baffling. The album came with a lyric sheet, though, obnoxiously, the words were printed en masse as a giant text block without punctuation. Years later, after I read commen-tary on the song and album, including Costello's own, I was able to piece together the song's cultural and site-specific details in such a way that evokes Continental disgrace, desperation, scandal, regret. But it didn't matter that the words were beyond my immediate comprehension. The song scored my intensely lived days anyway. "Great art can communicate before it is understood," says T. S. Eliot. How can something I don't understand come to mean so much? Can an ache and its balm be translated by the yearning stretch from F# to G# and back to E, even if the words among the notes are perplexing? Over the years stray lines from the song would come to matter to me a great deal—"The high heel he used to be has been ground down," "He's got a mind like a sewer and a heart like a fridge," and, especially, "You drink yourself insensitive and hate yourself in the morning"—unwelcome sentiments I was recognizing in myself and in my behavior toward some people close to me but, at this vantage point, decades from hearing the song for the first time, I wonder if those lines have grown on me over time, over distance, have come to penetrate in a way they couldn't have in my adolescence.

Anyway: when I listen to "Man Out of Time" now, I'm possessed of the image of me and that girl stepping from the bus that brought us back home from that New York trip, a late afternoon in late spring with rain coming down in sheets. We said *See ya* in teenage nonchalance, forced on my part, and that was it. That utterly ordinary, extraordinary moment—the pained inability to name and express feeling and affection—is evoked by a song that has nothing to do with my experience, that I still don't fully comprehend, written by an adult steeped in self-loathing, fumbling his way through public scandal and tarnished cultural history to find a way of interpreting his own louche and unhappy behavior in the public eye. On the other side of an ocean is me.

NOVEMBER 1966. SAM Moore and Dave Prater are in the Stax Studio at 926 East McLemore Avenue in Memphis. They're running through an arrangement for a new song written by Isaac Hayes and Dave Porter, who are also guiding and arranging the session for which the Stax house band, Booker T. & the MG's, are poised.

There is some dispute as to the origins of "When Something Is Wrong with My Baby," one of the most powerfully persuasive love songs of its era. In *Soulsville U.S.A.*, Rob Bowman recounts that the lyrics were crafted by Porter "while he was married to a woman whom he had impregnated when they were both still in high school."

> "I was quite honestly miserable with her," sighs Porter. "There was no love there. In the early part of my career I would fantasize about a lot of the things that I would come up with for my lyrics. I was in bed one night feeling miserable. Big house and a big car but I'm not in love and I'm not happy. I was fantasizing about what it would really be like to be in love. I got up out of bed and went downstairs and said, 'If I was in love with somebody then the relationship should be such that if

something is wrong with her, something is wrong with me.' It was about two o'clock in the morning and I wrote the whole song." Porter called Hayes at nine the next morning, sang it for him over the phone and said, "Man, we got a smash."

More recently, Robert Gordon in *Respect Yourself: Stax Records and the Soul Explosion* notes that Hayes remembered the song's genesis quite differently. "One day David and I were tired, went home, and David's wife at the time, he sat in the easy chair, pondering and toiling, and she said, 'What's wrong? Is something wrong with my baby?' David jumped up and he rang me. 'I got it, I got it.' Tired after a whole day's work, he got that inspiration and fired me up, came to my house, and we wrote 'When Something Is Wrong with My Baby.' Sam and Dave came in—another hit record!" Regardless of who's telling the truth here, the song transcends its origins. And by the time Moore and Prater, fully rehearsed, got around to recording the song on November 15, 1966, they were inside of it, and the genesis of something so eternal was beside the point. Gathering with the band—Booker T. Jones on organ, Steve Cropper on guitar, Donald "Duck" Dunn on bass, and Al Jackson on drums; Hayes added piano, and the Memphis Horns were there, too—Sam & Dave tell us that it doesn't matter whether the song issued from fantasy or from reality, from loss or from gain; what matters is the story it tells.

"When Something Is Wrong with My Baby" begins minimally, in an almost childlike way, with four strums from Cropper's and Dunn's guitars, the simplest of chimes. After a double-time figure from Dunn, the verse begins with quietly descending piano triplets from Hayes, a bar before Moore enters to sing in front of the Stax band at their most economical—which is saying something. Is it possible for a band to play notes and for those notes to disappear, leaving behind only the traces of those notes to be recorded? That's what it sounds like is happening in the studio on this day. The band's playing, restrained to the point of nearly vanishing, is all Sam & Dave need, all that the story needs to be heard; the Memphis Horns that acquiesce throughout never get showy because they don't have to. (On occasion, I run to the liner notes to assure myself that, yes, Al Jackson does appear on this song, so subtle and unadorned is his playing; was he recorded behind camouflage?) Booker T. & the MG's knew in their collective heart that sometimes a band can get in the way. They get out of their own way on their quietly propulsive "Groovin'" from 1967 and still deliver a muscular performance—such were the enchanted physics at work at Stax Studio in the mid-1960s.

The story's summed up in the song's title, and essayed in the chorus: *when something is wrong with my baby, something is wrong with me*. This simple but vast discovery—that when your loved one is down, so will you be—I'd acted out before, dutifully, with other girls, with good intentions, but onstage, in front of footlights. Now when I listen to this song I hear what I never heard, or couldn't hear, during earlier years. When I rediscovered "When Something Is Wrong with My Baby" after I'd been with Amy for a while, I thought: yes, this is love, helplessly. Moore and Prater, responding to Hayes and Porter, know and sing with deep gratitude. They address the song to an unknown other who might be doubting the relationship, because "she's no good." Sam & Dave respond, "she's my woman and I know I'm her man." Their confidence is palpable, and moving, and, as in all of their greatest performances, Moore and Prater sing as if they're one man, navigating the conflicts and harmonies of pride, confidence, and endurance. (Never mind that their private lives were often in vivid conflict with romantic fidelity—see Dave Marsh's *Sam and Dave: An Oral History*.)

The chords are fairly simple, and the melody embellishes what's left uncomplicated in the arrangement. Moore begins the song alone, somewhat tentatively, and offers the title as a statement, a sales pitch; we don't have to believe him. I didn't. And then Prater enters to sing the two-line bridge, a characteristic, gruffly sung refinement of his partner's message—*We've been through so much together / We've been as one, and that's what makes it better*—and the two, in touching unison, bring us to the chorus. The stirring changes in the bridge and the return to C for the chorus crack a code: now as they sing the title, it means something impossibly profound, as if the song has somehow aged and matured in one minute. It's not a Hallmark sentiment, what an affected child says. On the well-worn path of verse/bridge/chorus, Hayes and Porter, as warmly, knowingly translated by the masters Sam & Dave, clarify the breadth and maturity, the value and empathy of an adult relationship. It takes one minute and twenty-three seconds in the song before an epiphany glows; it took me years to turn toward that radiance, where with me, having arrived on her own rocky terms, was Amy. "Oh, you just wouldn't understand," Sam & Dave sing. They're singing to the doubters, but as I listen they're singing to me, the naive kid from years ago.

In the early 1990s, Elvis Costello wrote "Why Can't a Man Stand Alone," a prideful paean to independence written (like "When Something Is Wrong with My Baby") in 6/8 time, and offered it to Moore. The song was seemingly well-suited for him, but he passed.[4] "It's easy to theorize songs for people, but they don't always work out. For instance, I wrote 'Why Can't a Man Stand Alone' for Sam Moore, but he didn't take it," Costello admitted to Laura Emerick. "Now when I think about it, the song has too many words." He added, knowingly: "Sometimes lyrics can get in the way of expression." Indeed. The greatest line in "When Something Is Wrong with My Baby" might occur in the second bridge, a wordless "Oh oh oh oh" from Sam Moore, crying and comprehending.

---

4 "Why Can't a Man Stand Alone" eventually appeared on Costello's 1996 collection of songs written for other artists, *All This Useless Beauty*.

PETER HANDKE, FROM his essay "The Jukebox":

> In listening to a jukebox he was never beside himself,
> or feverish, or dreamy, as he otherwise was with music
> that affected him—even strictly classical music, and the
> seemingly rapturous music of earlier, preceding eras.
> The dangerous part about listening to music, someone
> had once told him, was the propensity it had to make
> one perceive something that remained to be done as
> already done. The jukebox sound of his early years, on
> the other hand, literally caused him to collect himself,
> and awakened, or activated, his images of what might
> be possible and encouraged him to contemplate them.

It's the late 1980s, and Handke's writing about his experiences writing about (or more accurately, not writing about) an essay on jukeboxes, those beloved, magical "music boxes" of his adolescence that signaled mystery and clarity alike. Writing in the distancing third person, meandering among writer's block, ennui, aimless traveling across eastern Europe, and sundry distractions, Handke navigates the irrational and substantial pleasures created in a tavern by a gleaming machine loaded with scratchy vinyl.

A bit later in the essay he describes a transcendent experience commencing with "the measured, positively ceremonial act of 'going to push the buttons.'" It's late winter, somewhere in the past; he's in a jukebox café, reading, trying to work, but

the jukebox has other plans. "This café was in a rather untypi-
cal location for such places," he writes, "at the edge of the city
park, and its glass display cases with pastries and its marble-
topped tables were also incongruous."

> The box was playing, but he was waiting as usual for the
> songs he had selected; only then was it right. Suddenly,
> after the pause between records, which, along with those
> noises—clicking, a whirring sound of searching back
> and forth through the belly of the device, snapping,
> swinging into place, a crackle before the first measure—
> constituted the essence of the jukebox, as it were, a kind
> of music came swelling out of the depths that made him
> experience, for the first time in his life, and later only
> in moments of love, what is technically referred to as
> "levitation," and which he himself, more than a quar-
> ter of a century later, would call—what? "epiphany"?
> "ecstasy"? "fusing with the world"? Or thus: "That—
> this song, this sound—is now me; with these voices,
> these harmonies, I have become, as never before in life,
> who I am: as this song is, so am I, complete"? (As usual
> there was an expression for it, but as usual it was not
> quite the same thing. He became one with the music.)

A JUKEBOX CAN narrate an evening, a long afternoon, or
a moment, playing songs that we choose, songs that we're

surprised by, songs that we're ready to listen to again and again, or that we're unwilling to hear. Of the many jukeboxes in front of which I've levitated—at Delilah's in Chicago; at the International in New York City; the one at Millie & Al's in Adams Morgan, Washington D.C., that inexplicably played for free one long fantastic night in the 1980s; the one at the late, lamented Lakeside Lounge in the East Village stocked by the matchless James "The Hound" Marshall—I have perhaps the greatest affection for the jukebox that glowed in the Union Bar and Grill in Athens, Ohio.

In 1961, singer Patsy Cline was emerging from a lengthy commercial dry spell, difficult now to imagine of a gifted, iconic artist made preternaturally timeless and influential via her early, tragic death. Since the mid-1950s she'd been releasing singles on the Pasadena-based 4 Star Records label but, with the exception of "Walkin' After Midnight" and its flipside, "Poor Man's Roses (Or a Rich Man's Gold)," released in 1957, none had charted on either the country or pop *Billboard* charts. In 1961 her fortunes changed, thanks to two suddenly popular singles, Hank Cochran and Harlan Howard's "I Fall to Pieces" and Willie Nelson's "Crazy," which peaked on the country chart at numbers one and two, respectively. Cline, frustrated but single-mindedly devoted to her craft and career, and signed now to Decca Records, had agreed to stray from her beloved honky-tonk toward the more pop-leaning, commercially viable "Nashville Sound" in the hands of producer Owen Bradley and

Nashville's "A-Team" of ace studio musicians. If you were near a transistor radio in the early months of 1962 and heard "She's Got You," Cline's follow-up to "Crazy," you recognized the harmonies of the Jordanaires from Elvis's recent hits, though you probably wouldn't have known their name. Their sweetly decorous tones over the simple, two-chord opening, the twinkling piano, announce a wholesome song, one that's hopeful at keeping loss and grief at arm's length.

And then Cline begins to sing. Though, really, she's continuing to sing the song she was introduced to in her kitchen from a week earlier. Eager to be the one to compose (and to cash in on) Cline's next single, Cochran called her excitedly after he'd written the song, inspired by the melancholy image of old photos in his desk in his writing studio, and composed in ten minutes. After stopping at a liquor store for Cline, he hurried to her house on the west side of Nashville and assured her with confidence that he'd written a big one. According to Ellis Nassour, Cochran and Cline sat in her kitchen, opened the bottle, and by the time Cochran played the simple, devastating song and Cline learned it, the two were helpless with tears. There's an image: Hank Cochran and Patsy Cline weeping under the kitchen light, a guitar, a drained bottle, an eternal song echoing off of linoleum floors and the icebox.

Cline phoned Bradley and sang "She's Got You" to him down the line. The producer knew at once that it was a score, and he ushered her into the studio the next week. On

December 17, supported by the Jordanaires, Harold Bradley on bass, Floyd Cramer on piano, Murrey "Buddy" Harman on drums, Walter Haynes on steel guitar, Randy Hughes on acoustic guitar, Grady Martin on electric guitar, Bob Moore on acoustic bass, and Bill Pursell on organ, Cline recorded "She's Got You" over three hours at the Quonset Hut Studio at 804 Sixteenth Avenue South, in Nashville. That's a lot of musicians creating music that I have to remind myself is actually there. All I hear is Patsy, her throaty contralto so resonant that the affecting leap to the word "different" in each verse—the song's highest note and the bruising discovery around which the song turns—feels willed against will, unavoidable, enormous. In under three minutes, cherished mementoes, warmed by affection and sentiment—a clutch of photographs, a stack of 45s, a class ring—are forlornly recognized as things, simply, paltry stand-ins for the passions the giver is now giving elsewhere.

Cline's biography has been shared often: her father abandoned the family when she was in high school; her devotion to singing and her art bore her through a meager upbringing, an unhappy first marriage, a devastating automobile accident that nearly killed her, commercial pitfalls, and vexed recording sessions. "She was a hurt individual, a great cut-up on the outside but hurting on the inside." So observed Lightnin' Chance, the venerable mid-century Nashville session bass player, to Nassour. "Some of it went back to her childhood when her father deserted the family. We got into this minutely, talking in the back of those cars, going from date to date. The secret behind Patsy was how she lived every note and word of her songs." Chance recalls recording "A Church, a Courtroom, and Then Goodbye," an early Cline side. "There was a line—it's the only one I remember—that told how she hated the sight of that courtroom where man-made laws pushed God's law aside. You could feel the hate and bitterness, her own experiences. Patsy had a story to tell, and nobody ever knew what it was. If there were parallels in her music, she had a way of identifying with them."

I willfully ignored them. The jukebox at the Union often played Cline's greatest-hits album, and I was often there to hear. The perpetually lurid low-red glow of my beloved bar shadowed a nightly blend of graduate students, townies, and misfits, and my friends and I would close the joint Thursdays through Sundays. I was 350 miles away from my college girlfriend and, loosened by the distance, began a relationship with N., a fellow grad student, borne of attraction, the bunker mentality of new, scared M.A. candidates, and, mostly, booze. That I was cheating on my long-term girlfriend was rarely acknowledged directly, and, besides, the pleasure of waking up in a different girl's bed, the indulgences of newness, made it too intense and fun for me to care much. Flash forward to Columbus, Ohio, on a long beery evening with friends: N. entwined her hand into mine as we weaved up High Street; one day at school I walked into the graduate students' office to see her wearing my dad's vintage sweater that she'd borrowed from my closet without telling me; one too many private and meaningful glances across the bar. These were intimacies I didn't want, and which I courted in a reckless, juvenile way. By the time the quarter ended, I'd pulled away, and I returned to my girlfriend in Maryland to spend Christmas, hopeful to wish away the messiness of the previous few months.

When I returned to Athens, obnoxiously cool toward N., and was again holed up in the Union, a buddy told me that over the break she'd confessed to him of her nights soaking in her tub, while she played "She's Got You" on her stereo over and over again, thinking of me and what could've been. When I heard this, I shrugged. I knew the song, of course—we all knew it by then, and loved it every night it played along with Van and Jerry Lee and the Beatles and Sly and so many others now lost to the vapors—but I hadn't lived it. Even now I try to let myself off the hook: I was unwilling to hear the song's truths, so cavalier was I to the woman and to what she was feeling.

The "You" in the song is a direct address; Cline's singing to the man who left her. How that narrows the gap between the two of them! He's not a "He," distant and mythic; she's look-ing at him—is he in one of the photographs? Is she gazing at him across a bar as the jukebox plays, the way N. gazed at me? Are they the only two in the room?—and singing to him, their heartbreaking nearness made palpable. Elvis Costello (who now seems a Greek chorus in this essay on bafflement, clarity, and malice) recorded "She's Got You" twice in 1981 during the Nashville recording sessions for his *Almost Blue* album; he also performed it live that year on a George Jones HBO special. Costello changed the song's pronouns, singing "He's Got You." Had I heard his version during these messy years, even the switch to the culpable male perspective wouldn't have landed, so committed was I to drunkenly avoiding my responsibilities. Hank Cochran was tuned in: a year after Cline's death he wrote "A-11" (Buck Owens recorded it for his *Together Again/My Heart Skips a Beat* album in 1964), a tune where the singer begs the guy up at the jukebox not to select A-11. "This used to be our favorite spot," he laments to his shot glass and whoever will listen. "And when she was here it was heaven. It was here she told me that she loved me. And she always played A-11."

Someone hearing "She's Got You" in the Union the night before I did, or the following night, or last week, listened, or didn't, allowed the song in, or resisted it. Sometimes we hear songs in bars that, after Handke, move us so intensely that we feel loved, or that we're in love; sometimes we hear songs that bring us back so cruelly to life that we cover our ears, or talk loudly to strangers or ourselves to cover the noise. Sometimes we hear a song that means everything to those in the world with heartache, and nothing to the sour, childish ones who refuse to hear it. When I listen to "She's Got You" now, I am utterly, absurdly moved. The marriage of the simple melody and arrangement and Cline's wide, adult voice, the controlled loveliness of her cry, dissolves me, and I'm again witness to the transformative power in art. In my early twenties I was too ungenerous, though hardly immune to sentiment. (Please don't read the poems I wrote then.) My shrug at the knowledge that N. had spent much of her time away from me unhappy was posturing on my part, as, no doubt, the weeping in a bathtub listening to Pasty was, in some measure, dramatic on her part. Mine was a pose that deflected the song, sent it elsewhere, beyond my range of hearing, to the outer limits of wisdom. I was unwilling to step in the shoes of another.

On March 23, 1962, a year before her death, Cline performed "She's Got You," along with "Crazy," for the Grand Ole Opry, of which she'd been a member for two years. Sponsored by Pet Milk, her performance was recorded at WSM's Studio B in Nashville. Played live, the song retained a hint of Cline's honky-tonk past; it's still pop, but rustic and spunky around the edges, Marvin Hughes's piano galloping relative to Floyd Cramer's restrained playing in the studio. And Patsy responds. She's filmed from the waist up, wearing what I think is a brocade dress with a stiff, stylish collar, belted at the waist; her hair is sprayed firmly in place, her eyebrows are starkly painted, her lips are full, and she's sporting the glittery headband she often wore after her car accident to help relieve the pressure of intense headaches. Her hands are held decorously in front of her, one wrist ringed with a bracelet, the other with an incongruous black watch. She moves, but barely, swaying to the song's beat and despondency. The performance is superb, riveting really, given the unhappy foreknowledge of her imminent canonization. Her trademark "sobbing" catches in the phrase "The *only* thing new" are so moving as to reveal everything that her polite, affected television face masks. Perhaps because she was born one month after my mother, I feel a rebuke in Cline's singing in this performance, some lesson that I'd boyishly scorned. She sings the song's greatest lines, lines that could've been said by anyone in time reckoning with the unwanted burdens of memory, carefully, as if she's struck by their profound simplicity, their old newness, every time: *I've got your memories, or do they have me?*

PICTURE A BLACK-AND-WHITE Bill Owens photograph from one of his suburbia books. I'm an early teenager at a local garage sale, minding my younger brother, doing all I can to behave dutifully when all I really want to do is duck under this table and leaf through the cardboard box of thick, heavy *Playboy*s I've spied. But I remain in charge, find myself at a table stacked with old albums, and, flipping through, am quickly caught short by the mod avocado- and forest-green colors of the cover of Sam & Dave's *Soul Man*. I knew and loved the Blues Brothers' hit from a couple years back, and I dig the striking Stax logo and the skinny suits and porkpie hats that Sam & Dave are rocking on the front and back covers. I speak the song titles aloud: *Broke Down Piece of Man*; *The*

Good Runs the Bad Away; *Rich Kind of Poverty*; *I've Seen What Loneliness Can Do.* . . . Pull back, a wide shot: a skinny kid, muttering something, surrounded by the sunny cast-offs of suburban idyll. He'll buy that record for a quarter, take it home, play it on the family stereo, and, past the roadblocks of scratches and skips, will begin to mouth along to sounds, words, ideas, truths beyond his ken, adult stuff that, while the impossibly tight and funky groove of the album will forever delight and keep him moving, will stop him in his tracks one day, when he's ready to listen.

ORIGIN STORIES

I'M TEN OR eleven and it's a Saturday morning and again 10cc's "The Things We Do for Love" is on the radio in my bedroom or in my head; it's playing somewhere everywhere that bright suburban day and now it's become for me the aural equivalent of sun and warm afternoons not yet embittered by dusks, of June allowance walks and bike rides and woods swallowing me in the dark with a playground at the other end—and accompanying the song is Saturday's olfactory mascot, lemon Pledge, the sounding start of my mom's workday cleaning a house of eight people and a shedding dog, and now 10cc and lemon Pledge are entwined forever, nothing less than knowledge of adolescent freedom, nostalgia!—but if I think a little harder: the rue of sentimentality, of blitheness, of the dangers of trusting a mawkish memory of a boy lying in bed waking up to a buoyant pop song and a striped T-shirt in the drawer and a limegreenyellow world where drudgery and thanklessness evaporate and leave no trace, no clues yet to sorrow.

STEADY RAIN AND the station wagon was a submarine, how many leagues under, as we were on the way to a piano lesson at Mrs. P's, music important even then, a drive through slick winding roads after school let out, through and into neighborhoods I'd only see for these lessons, homes I wouldn't trick-or-treat at, windows I wouldn't glance into while walking home from school, guessing at the lives inside but mostly shuddering at the infinity of it all, thathomelikemine thathomelikemine thathomelikemine until it became too much, too heavy, this pre-knowledge that the unknowable stuff going on inside my own home was reproduced in their unknowableness in other homes, so I'd slide farther down in the forest green seat as my mom drove us to the lesson when I'd rather be home in front of the TV or down in the basement with a paperback, but resolutely the submarine made its way where what awaited me was a glimpse of Mrs. P's husband in the hallway at the top of carpeted stairs (*where are their kids?*), the exotic smells so strange and the weighty sense that this is a home, too, like mine and not like mine, and when my fingers later rested on middle C and I tapped out "The Birthday Party" or "Sandman's Near" or "Song of the Volga Boatmen," the focus on something helped, Mrs. P standing over my shoulder, soft and perfumey, the major and minor notes a lesson in changing faces and shifting moods I didn't understand yet understood, the rain outside falling calmly now, a soft curtain that if only for an hour or so drew together all of these odd, unfamiliar homes.

IN THE SUMMER I may have been cooled in the basement
by the central AC but my imagination was feverish as Heart's
"Crazy on You" spilled in all of its wildness from the radios at
the public pool and from the stereo in our rec room, though I
was young and didn't get the sex of the refrain or feel the tensions tightening in the majestic move from the verses to that sex
in the refrain, but the song got in me and stayed, was working
to amp up my fever without my knowing, and it's been there at
a kind of low boil ever since, and I see my sister getting ready to
go out with friends, she's young that summer too, only fifteen,
but her fever's ahead of mine, leading her from our house to
other houses and to unfamiliar cars and to groups of girls and I
imagined it all that summer, her curves, her distance, her smile,
her glances not at me but at others, her talent at the pool table
in the basement training for something strangely adult, and I
wonder whether any of this is true, that is, whether any of this
is true of her or whether I've imagined for her this wildness
that the song so achingly scores—outside of her closed bedroom door, the magnetic pull toward boys, the memory of what
happened as I happened—whether too feverish, too romantic,
too nostalgic for reality to corroborate, but beautiful feverish
"Crazy on You" sings its own story of bodies unable to stop
colliding, and there she was and here I am, and, well, there it is.

LAMB AND LESTER

C HARLES LAMB AND Lester Bangs have little in common. Lamb was born in 1775 and raised in London, the son of a clerk; Bangs was born in 1948 in Escondido, California, the son of a truck driver, and lived also in Detroit and Manhattan. Lamb clerked for a living at the East India Company and wrote in his spare time for *London Magazine*; Bangs wrote mostly album reviews for a living, for *Creem*, *Rolling Stone*, and other magazines, and wrote all day and all night. Lamb was generous-hearted, compassionate, wry; Bangs could be a bad drunk, was sometimes mean, and was often aggressive. Lamb wrote about poetry and the theater; Bangs wrote about rock and roll. Lamb skirted direct confession while writing behind a persona ("Elia"); Bangs was nakedly autobiographical. Lamb died at age fifty-nine; Bangs at thirty-three. Lamb's editor and biographer E. V. Lucas called Lamb "the most lovable figure in English literature"; Lou Reed (among others) said to Bangs, "You really are an asshole." Lamb's colleague and rival William Hazlitt, that old misanthrope, probably had more in common temperamentally with Bangs than did Lamb.

There are some similarities: both Lamb and Bangs were unmarried and had no children; both suffered from mental duress; both practiced what they preached (Lamb wrote sonnets and a play; Bangs formed a band and released a single); both were passionate about writing; both deeply distrusted smugness and pretension.

Each wrote an essay titled "New Year's Eve." Here's the opening of Lamb's, which appeared in *London Magazine* in January of 1821:

> Every man hath two birth-days: two days, at least, in every year, which set him upon revolving the lapse of time, as it affects his mortal duration. The one is that which in an especial manner he termeth *his*. In the gradual desuetude of old observances, this custom of solemnizing our proper birth-day hath nearly passed away, or is left to children, who reflect nothing at all about the matter, nor understand any thing in it beyond cake and orange. But the birth of a New Year is of an interest too wide to be pretermitted by king or cobbler. No one ever regarded the First of January with indifference. It is that from which all date their time, and count upon what is left. It is the nativity of our common Adam.
>
> Of all sound of all bells—(bells, the music nighest bordering upon heaven)—most solemn and touching is the peal which rings out the Old Year. I never hear it

without a gathering-up of my mind to a concentration
of all the images that have been diffused over the past
twelvemonth; all I have done or suffered, performed or
neglected—in that regretted time. I begin to know its
worth, as when a person dies. It takes a personal colour;
nor was it a poetical flight in a contemporary, when he
exclaimed

> I saw the skirts of the departing Year.

It is no more in what than sober sadness every one
of us seems to be conscious of, in that awful leave-
taking. I am sure I felt it, and all felt it with me, last
night; though some of my companions affected rather
to manifest an exhilaration at the birth of the coming
year, than any very tender regrets for the decease of its
predecessor.

HERE'S THE OPENING of Bangs's, which appeared in *Village Voice* on December 26, 1979:

> Lately every time you turn around somebody's saying:
> "The '80s are coming!" Like at the stroke of midnite on
> New Year's it's all gonna be *different!* And when you
> tell 'em, "Come on, you know everything's just gonna
> keep on slowly sinking," they get downright *mad!*
> Spoilsports! No sense of social duty! It's true that I am

antisocial! But so is my whole crowd. When our fave
bar the Bells of Hell closed down a few months back
we all stayed in our apartments instead of seeking out
a new watering hole. (Perhaps suggesting that, like the
buffalo, we are soon to disappear.) I told my shrink this
and he said: "You're all pathetic." . . .

I suppose you think I'm being negative. All right,
if I'm negative you go tell *Mother* there's something
wrong with the womb! Ha, gotcha! Besides which,
as the '80s loom I suspect that my antisocial minority
will soon be a majority, and we'll have an antisociety!
Imagine that! Will Rogers the ultimate outlaw! And
what better time to inaugurate this ghost town than
New Year's Eve! Ring out the old, ring in the old! And
older and older. I ask you, have you ever had a New
Year's Eve you enjoyed? Of course not! Why? Because
you've persisted in this insane delusion that somehow
things are supposed to keep getting better, or that the
cyclical nature of the ying-yang means that the earth
is supposed to replenish itself or some such horseshit!
Horseshit doesn't even replenish itself. Do these sidewalks? This peeling paint, crumbling plaster, backed-up
plumbing? A replenishable landlord? Fuck no!

There are two directions in which extants can go: (a)
stasis or (b) decay. And New Year's Eve is the biggest

bummer yet, because we all go out with these expectations and get totally soused just so we can stand to be around each other because we've spent the late fall and winter's first blush sinking deeper into *TV Guide*, and now we're expected to positively revel in proximity to these globs of hideous humanity. So OF COURSE horrible scenes ensue.

AN ESSAY HAS elastic boundaries. What it cannot or will not do is up to the essayist. An essay starts as a blank blueprint for, say, a house; the essayist has no idea how many floors or rooms there will be, or if there will be an attic, or a basement, or on how many acres the house will sit. That is: an essay goes where it goes, forward, and back, and to the side, motored by the essayist's own thought engine. Elastic, a blueprint, a motor: If I've mixed my metaphors here it's because an essay is hard to define. Lamb's and Bangs's essays about the last night of the year share the propulsion of a voice illuminating shadowy corners of personal experience. Here I sit, Lamb sighs, Bangs grumbles: let's go.

IT'S INTERESTING TO note what two essayists can do with similar subjects. Joan Didion and Phyllis Barber both write about the Hoover Dam, Didion in "At the Dam" from *The White Album* (1979), Barber in "Oh Say Can You See," the opening chapter of her memoir *How I Got Cultured* (1992). Didion moves through her essay characteristically: her argument is thoughtful but spare, thesis-driven but questioning. "At the Dam" is brief, modest even, and asks more questions than it answers, though at the end it comes close to solving the dilemma, *Why do I keep picturing the Dam?* (Hint: it will outlast us all.) Barber is asking the same question, though she isn't aware that she is. Her piece is strikingly different from Didion's, obsessive where Didion's is cool, hyper-emotional where Didion's is intellectual, impulsive and segmented where Didion's is smooth and linear. The dissembling at the heart of Barber's essay—*I don't think about the Dam much*—is greeted skeptically by the essay itself: the image of a menacing cloud keeps floating to the surface, revealed to be a mushroom cloud from a nuclear bomb test that Barber witnessed as a child, out in the desert with her family, near the Dam. Her attempts to forget that unsettling night and its sinister connections to the Dam are subverted by an essay that insists, *You can't forget.* As opposed to Didion's deliberate attempt to understand the Dam's significance, Barber does all she can to look away, to block a memory. But that dam can't hold.

WHEN LAMB, VIA Elia, turns his attention to New Year's Eve and sets "upon revolving the lapse of time," he finds himself gravitating to thoughts of mortality, which is, along with self-examination, his essay's real subject. Lamb gets there by traveling backward: an admission of current regrets and self-loathing dissolves into a nostalgic remembrance of his adolescence, when thoughts of death were rare, and semi-understood. "Not childhood alone, but the young man thirty, never feels practically that he is mortal," Lamb acknowledges. "He knows it indeed, and, if need were, he could preach a homily on the fragility of life; but he brings it not home to himself, anymore than in a hot June we can appropriate to our imagination the freezing days of December." Soon enough after turning thirty, Lamb, who was forty-seven when he wrote the essay, began to feel the unhappy stirrings of his own mortality, and his antipathy toward New Year's stems from that holiday's tendency to bring gloomy thoughts to the surface of his thinking. He can only escape into memories of the child Elia for so long, at one point questioning the value, and the maturity, of pining for the past: "That I am fond of indulging, beyond a hope for sympathy, in such retrospection, may be the symptom of some sickly idiosyncrasy." (Take note, all essayists.) Soon enough the pealing bells of New Year's bring him back to the ever-diminishing present.

Lamb's joie de vivre and capacity for cheery sentiment rescue the essay from morbidity. "I am in love with this green earth," he gushes. "The face of town and country; the unspeakable rural solitudes, and the sweet security of streets. I would set up my tabernacle here." He adds, "I am content to stand still at the age to which I am arrived." Blind guesses at the afterlife chill him: he wonders, can you hug a ghost? Are there books there? Are *my* books there? Can I be ironic in front of angels? What about fields, dinners, drink, friends? Are they in Heaven or are they lost forever at death? Lamb grimly accepts that there are no answers to such questions, but we ask them anyway. This line of thinking leads to the most startling and affecting sentence in the essay, one of Lamb's great confessions: "A new state of being staggers me."

EARLY IN "NEW Year's Eve" Lamb gives vent to some pretty intense self-criticism, admitting to deep disgust with Elia:

> If I know aught of myself, no one whose mind is introspective—and mine is painfully so—can have a less respect for his present identity, than I have for the man Elia. I know him to be light, and vain, and humorsome; a notorious * * *; addicted to * * * *; averse from counsel, neither taking it nor offering it;—* * * besides; a stammering buffoon; what you will; lay it on, and spare not; I subscribe to it all, and much more, than thou canst be willing to lay at his door————— . . .

Ironically, and funnily, the invective's made more potent by what's removed—the asterisks, which Lamb coyly admits in his notes signified nothing. The reader fills in the blanks, by imagining the worst, probably. I always do, anyway.

Coyness and modesty disguised as vividness. Compare to Bangs, who enumerates his faults in epic, lurid detail. I don't know that there's a greater illustration of Michel de Montaigne's "obedient servant of naive frankness" than Bangs. His "New Year's Eve" is rollicking where Lamb's is measured, a confessional piece of raw, funny autobiography, equal parts arrogant, sheepish, profane, and semi-repentant. Bangs takes his reader along on a bumpy chronological journey through a decade's worth of New Year's escapades (the majority of which are actual; one or two are fictionalized), blurting out his ill-mannered, adolescent behavior, especially where women, sex, hard drugs, and loud, aggressive rock and roll are involved, which is on nearly every page. Bangs drags us along to bars and to parties in the suburbs and cities, and we're captive to his bulldozing narratives and boorish behavior, nodding, wincing, laughing, rolling our eyes.

What rescues the essay's considerable lewdness, even meanness, from fatal self-indulgence is Bangs's acknowledgement of his own weaknesses. Two sorry related incidents capture the guilt beneath his incivility: on New Year's Eve 1973, drunk at a party with his ex-girlfriend, Bangs dances dirty with the hostess. This upsets his ex, and "later in the car in savage ugly liquored sexual frustration I dug one of my nails into her wrist until it bled. She told me I was a sissy. I was." A few years later, Bangs commenced a period where he stayed drunk "and practically [took] up residence at CBGB's," where he "played the role of Bukowskian bohemian/artiste in ze big sitcom." In late 1979 Bangs hit it off with a British media writer at a party. She was spectacularly drunk, and at her apartment later that night after she passes out on the couch, Bangs robs her. "I dug in her purse for the vial, actually found myself looking for a moment at her wallet, either couldn't go that far or realized how silly this whole charade was, grabbed the fifth of Pinch on the way out the door, stomping down just a little meaner in my badass Frye boots. Still as tough and mature obviously as the '73 night of the famous fingernail-dig."

Bangs's decision to write honestly about his lousy behavior doesn't necessarily redeem that behavior. But I find his essay moving. Like Lamb, Bangs takes the occasion of New Year's Eve to take stock of himself, his caustic, self-mocking tone a flipside to Lamb's more august stroll through life's messiness, and no less human. Near the end of his piece, Bangs writes that New Year's Eve "just seems to bring out the worst of ourselves, probably deriving from repression of the clear knowledge that we're another year older and deeper in debt but ain't accomplished jackshit and in fact are likely backpedaling; hatred of the rest of the human race because they've got our number in this department." Feeling grim, he closes the essay: "The only alternatives to make are this 'human dignity' stuff are that old saw about crossing the International Dateline, total isolation (always a good move anyway), or perhaps most sensibly JUST GIVING INTO THE THING AND ACTING LIKE TOTAL WRETCHED DISGUSTING BEASTS."

Lamb hears pealing bells from church towers, Bangs hears the Bells of Hell; Lamb quotes poets Samuel Coleridge and Charles Cotton, Bangs the Ramones and the Dictators; Lamb's tone is nostalgic, his language searching, Bangs's tone is coarse, his language plundering; Lamb ultimately ends his essay in a robust, generous mood; Bangs is in a churlish, nihilistic funk. Two eras, two men, two essays. Both writers are candidly personal, but differently so. Lamb's editors note that his essay likely "shocked the moral sense" of his contemporary and friend, poet Robert Southey, who complained about the "absence of a sounder religious feeling" in *Essays of Elia*. Lamb's self-examination pales in intensity to Bangs's, but it can be argued that it's more rigorous and self-effacing, where Bangs's struts with bluster. And what of persona? Lamb was deliberately writing as "Elia"; was Bangs, despite his confessions, posturing behind a macho exterior? Their essays are wildly contrasting in tone, circumstance, and revelation, but they share the quality of allowing the mind its inimitable shape on the page, each attempt originating in reflection on a man-made date whose purpose is to look both backward and forward. The vistas in each direction are as wide as the men are unique.

HOW TO BE POWERFUL AND TRIUMPHANT AND LONELY ALL AT THE SAME TIME: THE MANY CHANGES OF GREG CARTWRIGHT

*T*HE EMPTY BOTTLE, on Chicago's west side, is filling up. I order a beer and a shot. The guy next to me is about my size. In the club's mid-dark, he's a body mass ordering a drink. If I'll remember anything about him it'll be his barely-there-ness, some politeness directed generically at the barmaid. I don't know who he is. He's there and he's gone.

An hour or so later, he's onstage. I can see him more clearly now, though he's bathed in red light and surrounded by a band. Dressed in a flannel shirt, ripped jeans, and deck shoes, he looks like a doughy fan who'd been given a chance to jam onstage. Or he looks like Bob Mould's little brother. Either way, it seems right to me. Onstage, Greg Cartwright is friendly, loose, passionate, and shy, a strange blend that works both to intensify and to deflect attention, as if once he sends a song into the air, he wants to disappear inside of it. The moody

tunes sung by this ordinary-looking guy tell stories of despair
and elation, romantic politics and personal failings, scored by
pre-Beatles melodies and chord changes, country yearnings,
garage rock pummeling, and R&B sweat and ache. He plays
left-handed, his eyes often turned down at his guitar, as if he's
really singing to the instrument and to the links among head,
heart, and the world. He doesn't talk much between numbers—
he'll maybe crack a joke about a botched lyric or a fucked-up
ending—letting his tunes say everything that needs to be said.
In any given song, his voice moves from screech to Neil Young,
from howl to Dave Prater, from raspy growl to Lou Reed. What
a difference a few feet of elevation, a guitar, and a clutch of
tragically good rock-and-roll songs can make.

"SERIOUSLY, IF IT weren't for my wife I would live in a
lean-to in a field with a pile of records. In the rain."

ON JUNE 29, 1971, the city council of Memphis, Tennessee,
voted to officially change the name of a three-mile stretch of
Highway 51 south, between Shelby Drive and Brooks Road, to
Elvis Presley Boulevard. Councilman Downing Pryor originally
wanted the entire stretch of the highway from Mississippi to
northern Memphis so-named, but officials of Bellevue Baptist
Church objected to their house of worship being located on
a street named after Presley. A sign was erected on January
17, 1972, a week after Presley's thirty-seventh birthday, at a

ceremony outside of Graceland, with Memphis Mayor Wyeth Chandler and Elvis's father, Vernon Presley, in attendance. Two months and one day later, Greg Cartwright was born in Frayser, a town of about forty-five thousand, a small peninsula between two rivers that converge into the Mississippi, a hub for industrial manufacturing that required access to the rivers and rail yards. Ten miles from Graceland, rough and tumble Frayser fell, as did much of Memphis, as did much of the country, under the long spell cast by The King.

Frayser flourished for decades. In mid-century, the International Harvester plant employed more than twenty-six hundred workers; the nearby Firestone plant and other industries brought more jobs. The area merged with the City of Memphis in 1958; schools and shopping centers proliferated. But by the late 1970s, the boom's reverb was diminishing. "The men in my family worked at Firestone or Harvester, and the area was very blue-collar until the general collapse, when all the jobs disappeared," says Cartwright. "When I was a kid it was like a small town complete with its own main drag, surrounded by more rural farmland on one side. The other side butted right up against downtown Memphis." Frayser's population began to decline rapidly after International Harvester eliminated 20 percent of its workforce in 1980. Another 850 jobs vanished from Harvester two years later, leaving the factory with half of the workforce it employed at its peak. In 1985, International Harvester laid off the remainder of its employees and shuttered the factory for good. Firestone, too, went dark. In Reagan's America and well into the Clinton era, Frayser moved from middle-class stability to economic volatility.

For Cartwright, music soundtracked a humid and difficult but oddly beguiling town. "My dad had a large collection of records, and music was always on in the house so I was subliminally programmed from a very early age. I remember looking at records with inner sleeves and reading all the lyrics. When I was eleven or so I began writing poems and arranging them to look like inner sleeves. Then, when I was about twelve or thirteen I caught the bug to play guitar. I had some of my own records and had access to all of my dad's records." The Cartwright family listened to the radio on Sundays when they'd clean house, dad too busy dusting and vacuuming to bother with the stereo. This was Cartwright's radio time, when he discovered what others in town were hearing; lingering too is a memory of riding in the car with his dad. "It seems vaguely pivotal. He made his own cassette comps of his favorite tracks and artists. We were listening to a tape of Mick Ronson–era Bowie really loud because his car had no air conditioning. The windows were always down because it's always hot in Memphis and the music has to be loud to overpower the sound of warm air rushing around your head. I can't put my finger on a song but I can point to that tape."

Cartwright's obsession with music began early. "When I was just six years old, I had a portable record player that I'd take with me everywhere I went. I inherited all my uncle and aunt's records that were at my grandmother's house where I spent most of my summers. She gave me all of their 45s, there was a lot of oddball Memphis stuff in there that you wouldn't hear on the radio anymore. There was just a lot of odd stuff in general in there." Cartwright's grandmother introduced him to the thrills and spills of yard sales and thrift shops, and such mining for gold became a lifetime obsession for him, but in Memphis the radio was his real education. "When I was a kid listening to oldies radio stations in Memphis you would hear Pop 100 things, but you would also hear local hits, like the Hombres' 'It's a Gas,' or the Guilloteens' 'I Don't Believe.' Those kinds of songs were really cool and really local. But the way charts worked back then was so different. Local radio really could be local. Things were different." As an early teen with one ear tuned to the garrulous and wholly unique history of Memphis music—from Sun, Stax, and American Sound Studio to obscure local unknowns, kids in basements and garages—and one ear tuned to the hardcore shows he felt obligated to attend at The Antenna, a punk club on Madison Avenue, Cartwright began to identify, and to identify with, his hometown.

"I feel really lucky to have grown up there because it's such a musical place, and there are so many great types of music that started there, or came to fruition there that were such a huge influence on me," Cartwright says. "As soon as I discovered one thing that blew my mind, I discovered something else that blew my mind, and then it really blew my mind that it came from where I lived! It's really an amazing thing. In the 1950s and '60s, the recording industry was exploding, and everybody in Memphis was trying to do it, and not feeling like they really had to conform a whole lot to anything in particular. You could just get lucky with any combination. You could totally make something in a budget studio, and if the right DJs played it and if some other DJ heard it and played it out of town, you could go from a regional to a national chart hit. And so people are throwing all these crazy things against the wall, you know? They're not attempting to sound cosmopolitan or anything, they sound like redneck people singing soul songs."

He laughs affectionately, as much at the silliness of the statement as at the truths it embodies. "There were no limitations. And everything's kind of blending together in this way. I get the feeling that probably a lot of regional artists feel the same way about their town. I feel like I'm lucky because Memphis was such a music town that it probably happened even *more*, the idea that, 'Hey, man, the kid down the street has a hit record, I can fucking make a hit record!' There was so much of that.

"In the 1970s and '80s, after Memphis was in its decline, no one had any expectations of what you had to sound like in a band, but everybody understood the references, the Memphis references. So it was a great place to find my way as a musician. What if I'd been living in New York, or Seattle, or one of those types of places at that time? I would've felt more expectation to conform to gain popularity, but in Memphis everybody knew you were never going to be popular so you didn't have that kind of pressure to do something that would put you over the top or garner a larger audience." The economics of the depressed city all but ensured that working musicians in the 1980s and '90s weren't going to pocket a lot of dough anyway. "It made it a little bit easier to follow your own path."

An avid and committed record collector, with thousands of 45s and LPs in his possession, Cartwright can by ear identify a record made by Memphians. "At one point I think Memphis had more independent small labels than any other place in the country," he marvels. "When I'm out hunting, sometimes I'll find a record where there's no address, a small-label thing. Even though there's no information that tells me, or a publishing company that I can connect to something I know, I *know* when I hear a Memphis record. I can just *feel* it." He adds, laughing: "Nine times out of ten I'm right, and in that 10 percent where I'm wrong, it's probably from Arkansas. It came from somewhere very close by!"

CARTWRIGHT'S HISTORY IN bands is vast and eclectic, testament to his tireless energy, his craftsman's work ethic, and his love of playing live and with others. His first stable group was

Compulsive Gamblers. Formed in the early 1990s with friend and partner Jack Yarber soon after Cartwright graduated high school, Compulsive Gamblers featured violins and fiddles and the occasional saxophone in addition to Cartwright's and Yarber's lo-fi guitars. The band released four singles before disbanding, unable to stay together after a couple of band members defected.

In the tradition of the Ramones, Cartwright and Yarber swiftly adopted the surname Oblivian and formed a band of the same name: the Oblivians played primal garage punk and became widely influential on the scene and the darlings of indie labels Crypt, In the Red, Sympathy for the Record Industry, and Estrus; sonic wanderers like so many indie punk bands, the Oblivians released material with each of these labels (and others). With Cartwright and Yarber on guitar and Eric Oblivian (i.e., Eric Friedl) on drums—the men circulated instruments among themselves, though never a bass guitar—the band pounded and snarled their way through dozens of singles, EPs, and albums (including a 2013 reunion). The songs Cartwright wrote for the Oblivians were generally beery and loud and snotty, and funny, but the decibel levels masked a songwriter with melancholy and melodies to spare.

When the Oblivians split up in 1997, Cartwright and Yarber, retaining their surnames, re-formed Compulsive Gamblers and released two albums, both more muscular and melodic than earlier Gamblers material, and more complex emotionally than the primitive rawk of the Oblivians. Among album releases, national and international touring, and bleary-eyed sound checks, Cartwright would meet his wife, Esther; they're raising three children, Andrew, Alex, and Ruby. He's worked as a cook, a salesman, an electrician, has owned and operated a record store, done landscaping, toiled at many nameless jobs using his hands that would rather be holding a guitar. ("I've tried my hand at everything that seemed reasonable for a traveling musician, and even a few that were clearly not. The most likely influence of any of these was my stint working at a bookstore. Not so much because of the books but because of the people who buy books. Or steal them.") This version of Compulsive Gamblers also fell apart—before the second album was released, in fact—and in the early 2000s Cartwright, following a stint playing too far from home in Toronto's rootsy Deadly Snakes, began jamming with a handful of Memphis-area musicians, working his way through new material that was vastly different from his earlier bands. After a few lineups came and went, including one briefly featuring Melissa Dunn, niece of famed Stax house musician and Booker T. & the MG's bassist Donald "Duck" Dunn, Cartwright settled in with a quartet.

He dubbed them Reigning Sound. Their debut seven-inch EP was released on Sympathy for the Record Industry in 2000. Cartwright's songwriting had found its truest and sturdiest home.

FROM STANLEY BOOTH'S *Rythm Oil*:

> "Dan [Penn]," I said, "what is it about Memphis?"
>
> "It ain't Memphis," he said. "It's the South."
>
> "Well, what is it about the South?"
>
> "People down here don't let nobody tell them what to do."
>
> "But how does it happen that they know what to do?"
>
> He twirled the ukulele by the neck, played two chords, and squinted at me across the desk. "I ain't any explanation for it," he said.

This small exchange, casual and epochal, has been passed around by many since its first appearance in a piece Booth wrote in 1966, and was also quoted in Peter Guralnick's indispensable history of Southern R&B music, *Sweet Soul Music*. It captures something essential about Memphis: the tension between result and process, which is to say between light and dark, which is to say between surprise and mystery. For years, Cartwright has been writing songs of love and loss, pleasures and regrets, that respond to his hometown and its particular alchemy of independent spirit and craft. "I continue to be influenced by the place I grew up and all the music that came out of it," he says, "as well as all the strains that passed through it, and were subsequently absorbed or evolved there. Especially all the ones that managed to slip through the cracks or were forgotten. They mean a great deal to me in a way I can't explain. They have great qualities, but they go unnoticed and unloved.

Somebody's gotta love the orphans, and maybe they have to love a little more."

Robert Gordon, author of celebrated biographies of Muddy Waters and Stax Records and *It Came From Memphis*—a boisterous cultural history of the city—considers Cartwright's career as echoing the diversity of artists and styles he grew up listening to on the radio. "The part of Memphis I hear in Greg's music is the end of the great AM radio days," Gordon says. "We had two great pop stations that played black and white hits, and two great black-oriented stations. In the '70s I'd sometimes tune into FM if they were broadcasting a local concert I was interested in, but it was past 1975 before my preference became FM. The AM had that great sense of pop brevity in its songs. They'd hit and run. Didn't like what you heard? Hang around for the next one. It would go from Beatles or Stones—the most popular of musics, to Motown and Stax to Detroit and Philadelphia and the U.K., to the oddity and glam—it just kept coming. AM was dedicated to the most popular music, but Memphis AM had a very serious commitment to diversity, with a foot firmly in the Memphis scene. On all four of the stations. There were more than four, but it seemed to me like only four. I feel like you get some of that in [Reigning Sound's second album] *Time Bomb High School*, in particular.

"And Greg is a serious record hound. When he had his own record store here"—Legba, which Cartwright eventually sold to Friedl, who renamed it Goner Records after the label he owns—"it may have been ostensibly about him making money in a business, but I think the true purpose was for him to hope that every record that was ever made would come through and that he would have the chance to play all of them from behind the counter. And short of that, at least the best ones would come through and he'd dive into those. It was research, in other words, and pleasure. And it happened to pay and to come with a rehearsal space in the back. Kind of ideal."

Gordon notes that Cartwright hails from a part of Memphis that produced many garage bands and great guitarists, "so there was a path he could follow. What's great is that, on that path, he blazed his own trail. He updated the sounds, often by tweaking retro sounds, imbued the music with his own personality, like all good artists do, and he found a supportive crowd—here at home, sort of rippling out from Midtown, to the wider region and soon enough nationally."

Gordon adds: "I saw him DJ a party once, and it was quite like listening to a great AM radio show. It was all over the place. And all exciting."

"IF GREG WAS alive and writing in the early '60s, I don't think he'd have any problems getting an office with a window in the Brill Building," said Mikey Post, Reigning Sound drummer.

TWO SIDES TO Every Man, Reigning Sound's debut 7-inch EP, surprised fans who were expecting the raucous garage punk of the Oblivians. Cartwright was conscious of expectations and, anxious to progress from two-chord din, presented his new songs as a sampler for Reigning Sound's debut album, *Break Up . . . Break Down*, released on Sympathy for the Record Industry in 2001.

Cartwright's saying, *Look, you're as likely to find the Everly Brothers and Harry Nilsson in my records as the Cramps and the Misfits*. The EP's three songs inadvertently laid out the major styles that Cartwright's come to explore in Reigning Sound. The A-side is "Here Without You," a haunting, mostly acoustic cover of a song from the Byrds' 1965 debut, *Mr. Tambourine Man*; the B-side features two Cartwright originals, "West Texas Sound," a hoarsely sung, driving garage stomp that he'd previously recorded with Deadly Snakes, less a song than an extended grunt, and "Pretty Girl," a casually exultant beat ballad with a chorus that scores an epiphany. The latter tells the story of an ordinary moment: a guy leaves a party with his girl; fumbling for his keys in the dark, he turns as she kisses him on the cheek and he's rendered speechless by the simple gesture and her beauty, a beauty he knew but never felt so strongly. Like Tom Petty in "Here Comes My Girl," Cartwright half-sings, half-talks his verses about the quotidian stuff—arriving somewhere, departing that place—until, struck, and startled, his chorus "(Sha la la la la la lee, the pretty girl's with me") bursts through the routine with lyric color: the barely-articulated surprise that a melody gives, or scores, or makes.

Joe King Carrasco once said, perhaps half-jokingly, perhaps deadly earnest, that all he aspired to in his career was to write a song as good as ? and the Mysterians' "96 Tears." I ask Cartwright if there's a song out there that he considers such an achievement, as something to aspire to. "For a rock-and-roll song, I hold Danny Burk & the Invaders' 'Ain't Going Nowhere' in pretty high esteem. It's a Memphis record from '66 or so but the vocal is super snotty and punk and the riff is so hypnotic that it almost resembles something from the first Suicide LP. It's a sound and an idea that really inspires me to make something equally powerful. I also really like 'That's Alright by Me' by Gene Clark. It's a late track for him but just as good as anything he ever wrote. It's definitely a vibe I shoot for sometimes, or at least a measuring stick for me as a writer."

A slab of homegrown hysteria, "Ain't Going Nowhere" was produced by Sun Records guitarist Roland Janes at his own Sonic Studio and was released on his Ara label in 1966. It's a brief and frantic twelve-bar blues, Jimmie Crawford's lead guitar bravely channeling Link Wray, drummer Eddie Sheridan's drums forging the rocky shore into which the whole thing, made of adolescent nerve, threatens to crash-land. Clark, a founding member of the Byrds, wrote and recorded "That's Alright by Me" sometime in the late 1960s after he'd left the seminal band, but the song wasn't released until after his death in 1991. Given an early Johnny Cash spirit in its plucked acoustic,

Clark's sing-along marries loss with acceptance ("I know you think you must go, that's alright with me"), though underneath that melody there are some anxieties. A salient line in the first verse must have struck Cartwright the first time he heard it: "my sensitivity is dying." Obscure '60s garage rock, and a folky, acoustic-band gem from a singer-songwriter. Ends of the sonic spectrum. What's in between except everything?

HERE'S A PARLOR game: try and distinguish Reigning Sound's cover songs from Cartwright's originals. There are usually two or three songs from other artists on each Reigning Sound album, historical templates, spirit cousins to the tunes that surround them. From the Beach Boys, the Everly Brothers, Carl Perkins, and Sam & Dave to the Guilloteens, the Carpetbaggers, Glass Sun, and Flash and the Memphis Casuals, Cartwright's covers range over the sonic map, touching on popular and obscure acts, nationally known and locally incubated. "What attracted me to Reigning Sound wasn't the original stuff but their and Greg's take on the Memphis '60s garage covers they did," says Ron Hall, Memphis music historian, record collector, and author of *Playing for a Piece of the Door: A History of Garage & Frat Bands in Memphis, 1960–1975*. "I was blown away by 'Don't Send Me No Flowers,' 'Stormy Weather,' 'I Don't Believe,' 'Brown Paper Sack.' They blended so well with the original stuff, many younger fans here thought they were original." He adds, "You have to be careful with a good songwriter like Greg, to overpraise the covers as opposed to his own stuff. But Greg seemed to enjoy the fact that I loved the stuff."

A record dealer in Memphis for more than thirty years, Hall has known Cartwright for a long time. (He discovered later that he and Cartwright's dad had attended the same high school.) Hall feels that, having grown up in Frayser, Cartwright had a different kind of exposure to the "Memphis vibe" than kids who grow up in the Midtown area. "To be frank, it was more of a redneck area so he was probably exposed to heavier rock sounds. His knowledge of the soul stuff is far better than my own. He went beyond who the artists were, he researched writers, producers, studios, wanting to know where the effects, warmth, vibe came from. I remember one night him coming to my house with a batch of records and him having cool west Tennessee bands I hadn't heard, but also knowing about small studios in the area where obscure soul stuff was cut.

"I was impressed by his passion to *know* about each record. I miss that."

GREIL MARCUS, FROM *The History of Rock 'n' Roll in Ten Songs*: "Regardless of who writes it, no successful song is a memoir, a news story, and no such song does exactly what its author—and that can be the writer, the singer, the accompanist, the producer—wants it to do. One must draw on whatever new social energies and new ideas are in the air—energies and ideas that are sparking the artist, with or without his or her knowledge, with or without his or her consent, to make greater demands on life than he or she has ever made before." He continues: "That is true for the songwriter; it's true for the singer. The song, as Louise Brooks liked to quote 'an old dictionary' on the novel, 'is a subjective epic composition in which the author begs leave to treat the world according to his point of view,' but the song, as it takes shape, makes certain things rhythmically true and others false, makes certain phrases believable and others phony—and someone speaking to the world by himself or herself is never solely that. Other voices, those of one's family and musical ancestors, other singers competing on the charts, movie characters, poets, historical figures, present-day political actors, are part of the cast any good song calls up, and calls upon." Marcus is describing the long, enigmatic route between experience and expression, between the "I" and the "We." Cartwright may be writing from the storehouse of lived experiences, of living people with whom he relates and collides, but those experiences, those real people, assume an abstracted, generalized shape, become silhouettes into which the listener can step and see that she fits.

"He's rooted in tradition without being slavish about it," says Alex Greene, guitarist and organist in Reigning Sound from its inception to 2004. "He can evoke decades of song craft, but steers clear of obvious clichés. One thing I appreciate is that there is a literary quality to the characters, images, settings, but he avoids the overly wordy writing of, say, Elvis Costello. He's more like Joe South. Smart, but earthy." Mikey Post: "What separates Greg from the pack is that every song he writes tells a story. There's a clear picture painted in every lyric. He doesn't make you wade through a bunch of flowery nonsense to get to the heart of the story. It's also the subject matter—love lost, love found, and all the joy and misery it brings. Everyone's been in love, and lost love in some way or another, so it's very easy to relate to his songs." Larry Hardy, head of In the Red, a Los Angeles-based label that has issued several Reigning Sound records, notes, "One thing I've always been impressed with in Greg's songwriting and delivery is his ability to write lyrics that are pretty emotional and vulnerable yet the way he sings it is completely powerful and energetic. He's written lyrics that are so sad and melancholy that they can move me to tears under the right circumstances, like after a bad breakup, but the way he sings them is so soulful and strong." Greene: "A big draw for me is Greg's voice. There are so many varieties of affected singing out there in the indie rock world that it was a tremendous asset, in my mind, to be working with an unaffected soul-slash-rock-slash-country singer. There is a great honesty in his voice. It's hard to come by these days."

"I mostly sing about the obstacles of being content," Cartwright tells me. "Not because I want to wallow in them but because they are universal subjects of meditation. Even joy itself is bittersweet at times. People immediately connect with that struggle." He adds, "Happy people don't need you to say you understand. As an artist I don't have much to say to happy people. And that works out great because they're busy being content. For the rest of us, coming to terms with rejection, failure, death, and the fragility of love is very important. Some people are self-conscious about these things and maybe they don't want to talk about them, but sometimes it just feels good to know you're not alone. Books and music do this better than possibly anything else." Cartwright acknowledges that he can't write outside of what he knows, "not convincingly. Everything I write is either about me or something that happened to someone I'm really close to. For the most part it has to be something that happened to me, something I've thought about a lot, or something I've felt. Most of it is things that have happened to me. Life gives you plenty of fodder for being sad."

"When you make a big mistake, it never leaves your mind completely," he said to Austin Ray. "It's always there to reflect on, especially when the sensation comes around to make the same mistake again and you think you'll get a different outcome. I've always got several strings of thought going on when I try to write songs. I could be thinking about something that happened to me, or a friend, twenty years ago, and also thinking about some conversation or gossip I heard in a bar. It's all those things converging, where, in a way, you jump from one to the other, and you can tell a story that seems real. I'm all for that. That's an aesthetic I strive for—something that's emotional but also crafted, at the same time, to be a good pop song."

DURING OUR CONVERSATION, Cartwright considers something and then laughs loudly. "A lot of people say to me, 'Boy, you're writing all these really sad songs, you must have a really horrible relationship with your wife.' No, no, no, no! In fact, I found that not until I got into a really good head space and was in a relationship where I felt really good about myself that I was able to write sad songs that I felt could really connect with people." He said to John Jurgensen, "I can write a handful of party songs, but I can't fill up an album with them. For whatever reason, the thing that I return to are the sad songs. Doing the sad songs allows me to be happy."

The paradox? "When everything goes wrong, love won't leave you a song," Cartwright laments on 2009's aptly titled *Love and Curses*. "And no blue melody could ever please me."

HE'D BEGUN SEEING Esther, and he wanted to write something to say to her how happy he was. "I'd been in limbo for a while, not really understanding what it was really about to be in love with somebody, and that somebody can help you. They can be kind to you, and you can be kind back to them, and it's such a wonderful thing. It's basically saying thank you for this experience."

He's describing "I'm So Thankful," a stirringly carnal song from *Break Up . . . Break Down*. The album is moody and despondent—check the title—quiet, downbeat, no rockers, an album that Alex Greene said "really captured the sadness of living in Memphis, more than any other record except perhaps Big Star." The closing song, bruised by all that's come before ("I Don't Care," "Goodbye," "So Goes Love," "So Sad") sounds at first weary, defeated, until Cartwright begins to sing, and the bitterness that you thought you heard turns out to have been something else, full with desire. The performance by the band—Cartwright on guitars, Greene on organ, Jeremy Scott on bass, and Greg Roberson drumming—is stark, compact, and powerful, and recognizes that the chorus ("Let me show you how much tonight") is so sensual that all they have to do is ride the offering. Beyond Cartwright's emotional, high-register vocal, the only drama in the playing emerges from the shadowy, urgent push of his guitar into the chorus—anything else would be too much, might turn this man's passion into something aggressive, a display of testosterone for his benefit, not hers.

"I'm So Thankful" is one of indie rock and roll's great love songs. Every time I listen to it, I picture Elvis on the other side of the studio, ghostly, singing "Power of My Love," from 1969. The correspondence is not unlikely: Reigning Sound recorded many of their albums, including *Break Up . . . Break Down*, at Doug Easley's and Davis McCain's McCain-Easley Studio, a nondescript, two-floor square building in east Memphis on Deadrick Avenue on a dead-end road near a Walgreens and an AutoZone. The setting is unremarkable, but the musical history of the building is pronounced. (It was harmed by fire in 2005, and shuttered; in 2009 it was reborn at another location.) Built in 1967 and known as Onyx (also as American East), the structure was the first in Memphis to be purpose-built as a music studio. It was conceived by business-man Don Crews, who'd been partnered with Chips Moman at the legendary American Sound Studio where over a hun-dred hits were recorded by, among others, Bobby Womack, B. J. Thomas, Dusty Springfield, the Box Tops, Joe Tex, Neil Diamond, and Aretha Franklin, and where Presley—riding his fabled "comeback"—cut "Power of My Love." Before form-ing American Sound, Chips Moman had been an engineer and producer at the Stax Studio. Follow the line on the map: Stax to Moman to American to Crews to Onyx to McCain-Easley. The cultural and aesthetic lineage winding its way to the back room in a tiny building on Deadrick Avenue startles.

In 1990, Easley and McCain moved into Onyx, remade it, and renamed it, ushering in an analog renaissance era for local and out-of-town punk and indie bands, recording in addition to Reigning Sound, the Grifters, Sonic Youth, Pavement, the White Stripes, and many others. Easley and McCain set up shop the same year that American Sound Studio was razed and replaced by a parking lot. "It had water damage, and termites had totally eaten the control room out. It was in really bad shape," McCain says.

"Power of My Love" is almost too much: too swagger-ing, too cocky, the dubbed-on female vocalists' soft-porn bor-dering on silly, yet the braggadocio is tempered by Presley's half-grinning lived-in vocal, and by the superb, muscular ensemble playing, especially by Gene Chrisman, the American Sound Studio house drummer, who helps transform what could have been merely strutty boasting into visceral, sensual confirmation. The recording captures the excitement going on in the room. The song was written by Bernie Baum, Bill Giant, and Florence Kaye, who, collectively or in pairs, had been responsible for composing many songs from Presley's Hollywood era, including some solid ones ("[You're the] Devil in Disguise," "Spinout") and some groaners ("Poison Ivy League," "Queenie Wahine's Papaya"). Apparently having inhaled the same redemptive fumes Presley did in 1968, they produced "Power of My Love," a lascivious song that Presley could believe in, revel in, have fun with, not out of contractual obligation but out of genuine joy. His song swaggers and brags, Cartwright's pledges and proposes, both originating in the body and in the body's promises of pleasure and gratitude. Singing at McCain-Easley, on the cusp of a career helming a great American rock-and-roll band, did Cartwright see Elvis, Moman, and Crew among the many Memphis ghosts?

JUNE 26, 2005. Reigning Sound is playing a set at Goner Records, the former site of Cartwright's record store. Cartwright has recently left Memphis and settled in Asheville, North Carolina; a positive move for his growing family, but in other ways unsettling for the River City native and devotee.

The band is supporting their most recent album (their third, following 2002's lively and rocking *Time Bomb High School*), a brutally loud record called, naturally, *Too Much Guitar*. The album was created by default: a clutch of quieter, more folk-rock songs had been laid down and mixed at Easley-McCain, but when guitarist and organist Alex Greene subsequently left the band to devote time to his growing family, Reigning Sound, reduced to a power trio, headed back to the studio, compelled to re-record the songs that had been reliant on Greene's moody, subtle playing.

One tune, "If You Can't Give Me Everything," was utterly transformed in the process, greedily exchanging downers for uppers. What began as a muted, Velvet Underground–styled kiss-off was amped up into a litany of vicious, desperate demands—"Get your foot out of my door!"—the chord changes moving from sleepy to torturous. You're surprised that it's the same song, yet you still believe that each was written by a different man. (Cartwright: "Doug Easley said, 'I liked it better when you were playing it slow.' And I said, 'Maybe you're right. Let's go back in and cut it, and slow it down to where it was.' The intended release was the slower version." These original quieter tracks were compiled, with several other stray songs, on *Home for Orphans*, released in 2005; a single from these sessions, "I'll Cry" backed with "Your Love," was released that same year.)

At Goner, some of the voltage is still sparking. Near the end of the set, Cartwright launches into "Two Thieves," a song he'd written while in Compulsive Gamblers, the final track on the Gamblers' final album (2000's *Crystal Gazing Luck Amazing*). A threnody for two of Cartwright's friends who'd died from substance abuse, "Two Thieves" moves among affection and disappointment, grief and frustration, and provides a chorus that's the very embodiment of sighing bittersweetness: *If the two of you had met, both your mothers would have wept—two peas in a pod, or just two thieves on the nod.* On the Gamblers' recorded version, Cartwright's voice is weary, unaffected; he's singing from the inside of discovery, and the discoveries are somehow both unhappy and celebratory. The band—Cartwright (Oblivian) and Dale Beavers on guitars; Jack Oblivian on drums; Brendan Lee Spengler on organ; Jeff Meier on bass—falls into, or it's more accurate to say that the song begins in the middle of, a Dylan/Band *Big Pink* murky mood; the musicians are tired-sounding, but alert, open to the possibilities of the newness of grief. The song's almost too painful to hear. In an exquisite, exhausted vocal that competes with a devastating slide guitar and that pushes at his top register, moving with and knocking against the simple melody and transcendent changes, despondent, searching for the shape the melody will make, Cartwright universalizes his experience with friends and lovers who are reckless and beyond our help. "Two Thieves" is one of Cartwright's most personal songs, and one of his greatest.

Wearing black boots, black slacks, and a black T-shirt, Cartwright plays backed-up against CD bins and band posters, standing just a few feet in front of the patrons who've come to Goner Records to see him and the latest Reigning Sound lineup (David Wayne Gay on bass, Lance Wille on drums). They get through the first verse and the chorus of "Two Thieves," played at an oddly brighter pace than the original, as if the band is willfully avoiding the song's sorrowful pull; Cartwright sounds distracted as he starts the second verse, he's pulled out of the song. And he abruptly ends it: "Hold on, I gotta stop," he says. "I'm getting electrocuted like hell. I don't know what it is . . ." Someone off-mike suggests that it must have something to do with the ground. A moment later, stepping to the front, chuckling, Cartwright says, "And with *that* we'll change mood," and he launches his band into the snarling anti-anthem "We Repel Each Other" from *Too Much Guitar*.

Too much. Cartwright, a formalist wrestling with the bedlam of grief. In *It Came From Memphis*, local legend Jim Dickinson says, "Memphis is about making chaos out of seeming order." In another world, poet Adrienne Rich: "In those years formalism was part of the strategy—like asbestos gloves, it allowed me to handle materials I couldn't pick up barehanded." *I'm getting electrocuted like hell.*

FOR YEARS, VIRTUALLY every day, he wrote out in his garage, on his acoustic, playing with chords, waiting to see what corner the next change will turn, what's there, always letting the music lead him to discover what he feels like talking about. Eventually, life broadened, deepened, became more complex. After the move to North Carolina, his teenage son took over the garage as a place to store his stuff, hang out, forge his own environment, as kids must do, and the house's sunny front room became Cartwright's workshop. "It's kind of apart from the rest of the house, so I get a little bit of privacy. If I have a day free and all the kids are at school I'll get out the four-track and sit and work on melodies and record things so I can have them to listen to later, try and work on them, push them a little bit further. Work out melodies and lyrics." His albums and 45s and music biographies are crammed into the front room, which is a plus: "If I want to take a break, listen to something, or if I have an idea that I'm working on and it pops in my head, like, *What would be something that would be a nice signpost of where this should go?* I can listen to it and it might inspire me." Once—if—he gets something going with two or three chords, he'll start humming a melody. "And once I have a melody line going, then I know what the lyrics should maybe do. Not necessarily what they should *say*, but at least what they should *do*."

I ask him what he means. "Once you come up with a melody, you can play that melody with any instrument, right? You can hum it, or you can sing it, or you can play it with a guitar, or a flute, or whatever. So you know what that melody's gonna do, but that doesn't mean with a vocal that you have to fill up all that space. You can either say a lot or say a little. You can fill it up with ideas or you can make it very simple, or . . . I don't even know how to say it." Here he pauses, trying to explain a mystery to himself. "Once you understand how the melody should work, then you start to tweak the melody and figure out if you have a rapid-fire type of lyric or if the lyric is kind of lazy or if the lyric is gonna be behind the beat with the melody. Once you understand the chord arrangement and the melody, then you kind of get into the nuances of what the vocal is gonna do. I might even graduate from humming something to actually singing something, just so I can see how the words set, you know, if the words should be long, or short, or how they twist around the melody. Those words may not stay at all. Sometimes they work out to where I actually use them, and sometimes I realize, *Okay I like the way this works, but this is not what I want to talk about.*"

Then what? "Well, it's funny. I can sit down and be in the mind to write one kind of song and play a couple chords and kinda get something going and then realize, *No, I don't think a major chord is going to work here, I think I need a minor 7th here.* And then I realize, *Oh, I'm not in the mood to write* that *kind of song at all, I'm in the mood to write* this *kind of song.* Once you get the juices flowing you never know what might pop out, because what your mood is right that minute might or might not reflect in the song you write. I could be just as content as can be and write something very melancholy. Sometimes it's even easier."

What does a minor chord do for you? "I love minor chords. They can be powerful and triumphant and lonely all at the same time."

IN HIS TWENTIES, serious about his craft, Cartwright faced a dilemma shared by many songwriters, post-1977: is there space for me in the anti-melody mayhem of punk rock, post-punk, and hardcore?

He felt the tensions early. "The first time I wrote a band name across the back of my jacket I was imitating what punk kids were doing, but I didn't know what punk really was yet, or who those bands were," he admits. "I thought you were just supposed to exclaim your love for an artist that other people didn't know or like or talk about. So I went to school with a jacket that said 'Nilsson' across the back. At the time, my dad was the only adult in my sphere who listened to his records so it seemed very personal." Cartwright felt and heard a certain punk attitude in the maverick Harry Nilsson—"There was something very dark there"—even if he couldn't name it. "The albums, they were really strange. Kind of quote-unquote punk, but pretty. I remember reaching my teenage years and listening to that song: [sings] 'You're breaking my heart, you're tearing it apart, so *fuck you*!' To a kid, you're just going, '*Yeahhh*! Curse words!'" When Cartwright grew up and listened to hardcore punk records, he felt "a little silly for equating my hero with this scene, but at least no one at my school could laugh at me, because they didn't even know what or who he was anyway."

Cartwright dutifully attended shows at The Antenna but as a bit of an outsider, acutely feeling the distance from his friends and peers who were punk and hardcore disciples. "That was a problem for me when I was in my early teens, and I started meeting people in high school who were into rock and roll," he admits. "I found out pretty quickly that they were into things I didn't know anything about. They were into hardcore and things that musically didn't really make any sense, stuff that was played so fast and with such abandonment of any concept of melody. I said to myself, *I don't really understand this, but I'm gonna go to shows.* And I'm not gonna pretend that I didn't understand some of it and that I didn't like some of it, but for the most part I didn't get it. I tried and I tried."

The bands and artists he did respond to were groups like the Cramps, Tav Falco's Panther Burns, the Gun Club, the Misfits, "things based on things that I understand and that I like. These people have figured out a way to put a new spin on all these traditional forms. And that is what I'm built for, because I can't do the other things. My heart really wouldn't be in it. I wouldn't know how to do it earnestly because I don't understand it. And that's not to say it isn't good, it just didn't click with me."

Doug Easley, whose partner Davis McCain was for years the sound man at The Antenna, has a wide-angle take on many young Memphians' attitude toward punk rock, an outlook that's steeped in the tradition and history of the city. "It seemed like Memphis punk happened, but the musicians couldn't really reject what had happened musically because they actually *liked* the past. Sometimes I think it's like Memphis was pissed because the rug got pulled out from under them when things died. We played the old songs in a new fucked-up way.

"Gotta stay current? Yeah, right."

SPEAKING WITH WRITER Fred Mills a decade ago, Cartwright observed that because his albums had remained under the radar, he hadn't had to deal with wide attention. "That keeps things right where I like it: I sell enough records so that whoever puts my record out will let me do whatever I want, but not so much attention that a major label would sign me to a contract where I have to do what they want me to do."

Cartwright has tasted some measure of conventional commercial success, most tantalizingly in 2007 writing songs for, coproducing, and playing on former Shangri-Las singer Mary Weiss's comeback album on Norton Records, *Dangerous Game*, a release that garnered positive reviews in major places (and landed an anxious Cartwright and band backing Weiss on Conan O'Brien's *Late Night*. "All these people asked me, 'Why were you wearing sunglasses? Were you trying to look cool?' And I reply, 'No. I was just so nervous. I needed something in between me and everything else.'"). But Norton, too, is a small enterprise run by devoted but cash-strapped owners.

Happily loyal to indie labels, Cartwright has had to weather problems endemic to them, such as poor distribution and limited recording and promotional budgets. Larry Hardy, whose label In the Red released *Time Bomb High School*, *Too Much Guitar*, and *Love and Curses*, was pleased with Reigning Sound's sales figures. "Their records sold well, by my label's standards, anyway. It depends on how you define conventional success. Greg's not really the sort of guy who is willing to go out and do a lot of the bullshit song and dance you have to do to get to that quote-unquote next level. I think it would sicken him to deal with that. I'd hope that he feels he's achieved success already. He has a lot of fans, respect among his peers, and he's doing his music for a living." He adds, "I think Greg's music ranks him alongside all the greats who came out of Memphis. He's incredibly successful in my eyes."

In 2014, Reigning Sound signed with Merge, a major independent label that has scored commercial hits with Arcade Fire, Spoon, and She & Him, and has issued critically celebrated, influential albums by Neutral Milk Hotel, Magnetic Fields, M. Ward, and others. Released in the summer of 2014, *Shattered*—recorded in Brooklyn, New York, mixed by old family hands down at McCain-Easley—features a new Reigning Sound lineup, with Post on drums, Benny Trokan on bass, Mike Catanese on guitar, and Dave Amels on organ (those four also play, sans Cartwright, as the Jay Vons). The bulk of Cartwright's songs on *Shattered*—there's one cover, Garand

Hilton's smoothly aggressive "Baby, It's Too Late"—lean heavily into Memphis's long, warm R&B and soul shadows, generally in the band's take on the Stax sound, and particularly in how they evoke the taut, economical, and expressive ensemble playing of Booker T. & the MG's. (The Stax band has long been a touchstone for Reigning Sound; original organist Alex Greene remembers telling himself, "'Okay, I'm going to pretend that I'm Booker T. moonlighting in a folk rock group.' I love Booker T. Jones's simplicity and sheer grooviness.") New songs like "In My Dreams," "I'm Trying (To Be the Man You Need)," and "Starting New" mine the effortless yet urgent, every-note-counts arrangements of the Stax sound, collapsing emotional turbulence and romantic chaos into charts and changes, the whole thing a melodic balance of passion and decorum. Other songs touch on sleek, '70s soul call-and-response grooves, rustic country strings, and rootsy pop.

Listen to "I'm Trying." It's song that I desperately wish I could hear Sam & Dave sing in some alternate universe, trading lines and pridefully exhorting each other. You half expect Cartwright to drop in a spoken section during the guitar solo—a clichéd arrangement would insist on it, and Amels gives the singer the organ-spotlight—but such a move would be corny here. Better to evoke the past, to let familiar notes and moods and arguments fill the empty spaces as Cartwright and his band go on singing and playing. Remember the young couple in "Pretty Girl?" That epiphany didn't take; they rarely do. The revelation of a kiss and the rush of her beauty faded—the next morning, in line with all of the others after it, and the days pile up, dragging regrets and responsibilities and all kinds of adult noise behind them. *All caught up on the things I said I'd do, If I don't pay enough attention to you, just know I'm trying to be the man you need.* The "sha la la la la la lee" that in an earlier time sang of surprise and gratitude is now gibberish from someone else's life. What's the currency of a kiss on the cheek in the dark? *Got no money or fancy clothes, but a true, true heart, I've got one of those.* He's trying.

CHICAGO'S BEAT KITCHEN, on another occasion. I'm waiting again for Greg Cartwright to hit the stage. This time, I know who he is. The opening band, the *third* opening band, is playing for a long time, their generic psychedelia and extended guitar solos casting a pall (over me, anyway). I turn to look past my shoulder to gauge the size of the crowd—it's packed—and there's Cartwright standing behind me, towered over by Dave Amels. Too shy to introduce myself, I turn away but not before I register a look on Cartwright's face of impatience blended with politeness. He wants to get onstage; he wants to sing. I wonder what he's thinking: the opening song? A 45 he scored at Salvation Army that afternoon? Some girl? He wants to go on and let loose his changes, let them please and surprise him and us again. He wants to sing. And now I picture him in dad's car. David Bowie's *Aladdin Sane* or *Pin Ups* is playing, all of the windows are down, and outside in Tennessee it's so hot that the roads melt and the trees sob, that old story. Cartwright's gone, wending his way among what the chords offer as promises, as surprises, as stories in the air.

BRAND NEW CADILLAC

AUGUST 1979

*Y*OU CAN'T KNOCK over a twelve-bar blues. Its deep roots run beneath mountains on the dark floor of the ocean all the way back to the USA, where girls want more but not from you, where new cars gleam, but when Vince Taylor and His Playboys' "Brand New Cadillac" was released in April of 1959, Paul and Mick were just four, Joe seven—cars were what you rolled along a bedroom floor, girls were a screechy distraction down the lane—and years later, Paul or Mick would see the 45, the bright red Parlophone label that said, that promised, "Made in Gt. Britain," and they brought the record home to their squat in Davis Road in Shepherd's Bush and spun it all the time (the B-side to "Pledging My Love," it rocked hard) and who were the Playboys? and how'd they get their name? and they were his, a gang: Taylor and his mates wore stiff black leather—Paul, Mick, Joe remember the photos from a magazine—and looked cocky as shit, teddy boys from the prime era of pomade, and Taylor, born in Middlesex, England, had even grown up in America, on both coasts, first in New Jersey then California (Hollywood High School!), and as a teenager before he returned to the U.K. he got a pilot's license, if you can fucking believe it, and flew up and into and through big blue American skies—you can't knock over a twelve-bar blues, so the guys would play the tune for kicks, using the song to warm up, meeting it halfway with cool irony, turning over the V8 in their loud, tight-as-chassis arrangement, working through its jumpy promises of excess and loss, Joe howling as if he truly believed the words, a dilemma sent by Taylor in a private anguished letter, while they filled in the jive-echoed looseness of the Playboys' arrangement with nerve and anxiety, desperate moves because this Cadillac's on the run, she's ahead now, and in the U.K. in the 1970s that car must've seemed as if it rolled off a widescreen from a different age, and if it's a metaphor and if she's with a better bloke who's got a better car, a bigger cock, well they'll speed up and still chase her as far as they can, desperate to unbelieve, until "Balls to you, Big Daddy!" because she's a tougher bird, and in the studio, caught up in this greaser fantasy—Mick and Joe playing off each other, Paul and Topper the thrumming and the pistons, the four of them riding the exhaust beyond Fifties Rocker Theatre that the song, stalled in lesser bands, can be reduced to—the Clash renew Vince Taylor and His Playboys for the Thatcher Era and dole queues, for the punks in line watching a Cadillac roar by in their imaginations, paying homage to America, to cars, to sex; at Wessex Studios, in London, they'd thought they were just banging through an old favorite, loosening up, aware that they'd caught fire and sped up by the song's end, a casual, exhilarating take that they'll revel in, but smartly fix, because work on the new album had barely started, after all. "It's a *take*!" shouts producer Guy Stevens. "All rock and roll speeds up!"

HUNTING LARRY HUNTING HANK

I love a great song, man. Oh yeah.

—LARRY BROWN

I'd rather be in a deep, dark grave
And know that my poor soul was saved
Than to live in this world in a house of gold

—HANK WILLIAMS

I NEVER MET CHIP.

"Oh, you've got to meet Chip!" The beaming young woman behind the check-in desk wears straight blonde hair and wire-rim glasses. "He was a good friend of his. He went fishing with him right before he died, I think. He'll be excited that you're here. I think he's working the third-floor bar tonight." My wife and I are in Oxford, Mississippi, where I've tracked down the late fiction writer Larry Brown's unfinished, unpublished screenplay of the life of Hank Williams, something that

I hadn't known existed until I came across a casual mention of it in an interview. I've driven 650 miles to read the screenplay.

"I've ALWAYS BEEN a big fan. We always had Hank Williams records in our house when I was a kid. I can remember my daddy singing 'My Bucket's Got a Hole in It.'"

That's Larry Brown talking, near the end of his life. He died of a heart attack on Thanksgiving Day in 2004 at his home in the Mississippi community of Yocona, a dozen or so miles southeast of Oxford. He was fifty-three years old, husband to Mary Annie and father to sons Billy Ray and Shane and daughter LeAnne. He'd smoked heavily for decades. He'd battled the bottle for much of his adult life, climbing on and off the wagon, enduring benders, more than once having been admitted to the hospital suffering variously from alcohol poisoning, stomach pains, and high blood pressure. He once overturned his truck on a rural road. He was always urging "just one more" to himself or his buddies at the bar, some of whom were his dear friends, some of whom were strangers, the latter usually young fans besotted with his art and his reputation.

Brown published nine books in his lifetime: two collections of stories—*Facing the Music* (1988) and *Big Bad Love* (1990); five novels—*Dirty Work* (1989), *Joe* (1991), *Father and Son* (1996), *Fay* (2000), and *The Rabbit Factory* (2003); and two essay collections—*On Fire* (1993) and *Billy Ray's Farm: Essays from a Place Called Tula* (2001); his sprawling, unfinished novel

A *Miracle of Catfish* appeared three years after his death with posthumous edits by his longtime editor Shannon Ravenel and Brown's own speculative notes as to his characters' and story's denouement. He wrote with deep affection and sympathy about marginalized characters, exclusively Southern, mostly blue-collar, the men and women you see leaving Walmart or a low-rent liquor store or a 7-Eleven who look worse for wear, generally scrubby, gnawed by shitty decisions and the clock. He invested in these struggling, often-overlooked adults and their innocent, wayward children and provided them with rich interior lives, the fecund north-Mississippi landscape a kind of rough corollary to human wild and animal instinct. I've loved Brown's work ever since I found *Big Bad Love* in a library sale more than a dozen years ago. His spare, elemental naturalism is at once pitiless and compassionate. Brown loves his characters, many of who live in borderline poverty under low ceilings of possibility, who collide with the worst aspects of themselves in a world that's indifferent to their suffering yet which, in its beauty, provides those characters respite and restoration.

Famously, Brown was a self-taught writer. Following a stint in the Marines during the Vietnam War, he worked various jobs, including laboring at a stove company, a convenience store, and Sears, sacking groceries, mending fences, cleaning carpets, installing chain-link fences, hauling hay, deadening timber, constructing homes. In 1977 he joined the Oxford Fire Department, and during his seventeen years there, he, a life-long reader, began writing fiction. He'd taken one creative writing class at the University of Mississippi, with novelist Ellen Douglas, but his long and solitary apprenticeship mostly involved studious, affectionate reading of Cormac McCarthy, William Faulkner, Harry Crews, Flannery O'Connor, Raymond Carver, and many others, and the unwavering labor of writing dozens of lousy stories and several poor novels, one of which he, despairing yet grimly sensible, tossed into a fire in his backyard. At the fire department on quiet evenings, and at home at the kitchen counter while his family slept, Brown sat at his wife's electric typewriter and wrote for hours and hours, forging a realistic outlook on the fates of his rural characters, honing in on a style of simple lyric declaration of personal chaos and the land's gorgeousness, and patient, sympathetic characterization.

He published his first story in 1982 in *Easyriders* magazine; over the next several years he wrote steadily, published haltingly, and fought raging fires at double-wide trailers and homes and campus buildings, witnessing harrowing images of ruin and destruction. He achieved success with his first collection of stories and landed at Algonquin Books under the enthusiastic and sympathetic championing of editor Shannon Ravenel. He wrote. He smoked. He drank and climbed into his pickup truck during many dusks, a cooler of iced-down Budweisers in the back and maybe a fifth of peppermint schnapps on the seat next to him, and he drove to the Oxford bars or aimlessly through the gloam of northern Mississippi on county routes 234, 445,

434, 331. . . . Mindful of his speed, indulging the soundtrack of darkening forests and cotton fields, the bright eyes of the deer and wild dogs appraising him from the edges of the woods, he considered his own demons, sang along to cassettes of country and blues, and drank.

At the age of twenty-nine, Larry Brown started writing fiction in earnest. At the age of twenty-nine, Hank Williams drank himself to death.

Williams died in the backseat of a car sometime on New Year's Day in 1953, somewhere between Nashville, Tennessee, and Oak Hill, West Virginia. His death surprised no one who was close to him. His drinking and prescription drug abuse had increased sharply during the final two years of his life, pacing the awful chronic pain in his back and the woes of his vexed relationships with his first wife, Audrey, and second, Billie Jean. His misery was as much public opera as private tragedy: his reputation as an alcoholic preceded him at every gig, from one-room schoolhouse to auditorium, and in August of 1952 he was kicked out of the storied Grand Ole Opry for habitual drunkenness. His no-shows escalated; when he did arrive for a gig late in his career he'd often have to be carried onstage and propped up to perform.

His suffering was at odds with his success: during his brief six-year recording career Williams scored twenty-two Top 10 *Billboard* country hits, all of them released on MGM Records, so many of them standard-bearers for the genre and timeless upon hearing that they seemed to have been plucked from ancient air, as if Hank was tuned to something eternal above the rest of our heads, even when he was cutting versions of other artists' songs. "Move It on Over," "Honky Tonkin'," "I Saw the Light," "A Mansion on the Hill," "Lovesick Blues," "Moanin' the Blues," "Hey Good Lookin'," "(I Heard That) Lonesome Whistle," "Jambalaya (On the Bayou)," "Settin' the Woods on Fire," "I'll Never Get Out of This World Alive," "Lost Highway," "I'm So Lonesome I Could Cry," "My Bucket's Got a Hole in It," "Cold, Cold Heart," "You Win Again": a jukebox of stark, unambiguous standards supported by the sturdy and unadorned backing of the Drifting Cowboys, sung by a man from a small town in south-central Alabama. Hank Williams's legacy was assured early.

Before he was in the ground he was myth, and his posthumous career was marked by reverence and capitalism. Much like Elvis Presley's, Williams's records have been reissued countless times in countless editions since his death, the early, cash-in releases marred by haphazard packaging and the application of saccharine strings and full backing bands, the more recent releases aided by scrupulous liner notes and respectful attention paid to the recording masters. Arguably, Hank Williams is the greatest country singer-songwriter who ever lived; among even casual fans his songs are Biblical in stature, and his early death only underscored the darkness, pain, and complexity behind the seeming simplicity of those songs, giving them additional gravitas, though they hardly needed it. "We have relied on Hank Williams," writer Lee Smith contends, to tell us "who we are and how we feel and what we hope for." There's nobody more gifted than Hank, she feels, "at capturing those essential elements of the human spirit: the anguish of lost love, the frustrations of love gone wrong, the hell of loneliness, the complexity of our feelings, the fragility of our relationships, our fear of death and belief in life hereafter."

Larry Brown was an ardent fan of country music and, thus, of Hank—lay a Hank song over a Brown story or novel and the correspondences reveal a thematic kinship. In stark, graphic ways, both men wrote about heartbreak, excesses, and the wearying struggle to live right. In a 1997 lecture at the Lafayette County–Oxford Library, Brown spoke about the head-lifting moments that books had always vouchsafed him, of "their ability to transport you to other times and other places through a journey of the mind," adding, "I've been able to share in these adventures through the power of the written word, and through the dedication of men and women who sit down at a typewriter, or a computer screen, or even a pad of paper and a pencil to try and render a piece of history or a shared experience in what it is to be human." Brown could well have been talking about the songs of Hank Williams.

"I KNEW LARRY when I lived in Oxford during the 1990s. I didn't know him real well, but we always spoke when we ran into each other, and he'd seen me play, so we usually talked about music." This is Tim Lee, a Knoxville, Tennessee–based musician raised in Mississippi who, with Bobby Sutliff, formed and played in the jangly roots-pop band the Windbreakers in the 1980s and early 1990s, before embarking on a solo career. "One of the first times I ran into him after we met, he was sitting in the cab of his little truck in a parking lot across from the Hoka Theater, listening to a cassette. I asked him what he was doing, and he started telling me about this band he was listening to. The way he talked about them and the times he saw them play, you could just tell this guy loved music. He felt it in a way not many people do." Lee adds: "Larry was just so fascinated by music, musicians, and especially songs. I loved listening to him talk about songs. The look on his face would change, as if he was in complete awe of the craft of songwriting. So it's only natural that he would gravitate toward the music of Williams. It was deceptively simple and straightforward, much like Larry's writing."

Lee happened to have been visiting in Mississippi for Thanksgiving when Brown died. He drove up to Oxford to attend the visitation. "Larry's pals had put together a soundtrack CD that the funeral home piped in that included a lot of Larry's favorites: Tom Waits, Lucinda Williams, Dylan, John Prine," he recalls. "His beloved Gibson acoustic guitar sat on a stand next to his coffin." Driving home the next day, Lee was inspired to produce a compilation of songs in honor of Brown's work, "because not only was Larry a big music fan, musicians were big fans of his. His was a mutual admiration society that included dozens of great players, singers, and songwriters." Lee envisioned the tribute album as "a mixtape of sorts, the type of thing that Larry would have enjoyed listening to as he drove his little truck into the 'gloam' with a cooler full of beer and an ass pocket of something that burns a little bit on the way down." *Just One More: A Musical Tribute to Larry Brown* was released on Bloodshot Records in 2007, featuring Lee, Bo Ramsey, Alejandro Escovedo, Robert Earl Keen Jr., Ben Weaver, Vic Chesnutt, North Mississippi Allstars, Jim Dickinson, and others, some of whom were friends of Brown's, some of whom knew him only through the characters he brought to life on his pages. "Larry absolutely loved music," Brown's wife Mary Annie commented at the album's release. "I think he wished sometimes that he had the talent to do music for a living. He always played his guitar every night. If he had to skip playing, he would always say he felt like the day was wasted."

North Carolinian filmmaker Gary Hawkins directed the documentary *The Rough South of Larry Brown* and was a close friend of Brown and his family, and he often played guitar with Brown when he'd visit Oxford, happy to have discovered another left-handed player who strung his guitar correctly. "After a few visits, Larry took to setting up the ideal playing conditions, just to be hospitable," Hawkins remembers. "We played music, and played other folks' music, and talked music, and went to see bands at Proud Larry's and other spots in Oxford. It seemed like everything sorta revolved around music one way or another." He concurs with Mary Annie about her husband's aspirations: "Sometimes, the thing you really want to be is not the thing you're good at, so you're stuck in an in-between place, and forced to choose, to sacrifice, and you feel for life that you've ignored something important, even if it was never there for you," he told me. "You're stuck with your apti-tude, which isn't necessarily your passion. Maybe that's some-what true of Larry, who wanted to sing and play but had no real gift for music. He was amazed by music, by its power, but he couldn't produce it. Not the way he could produce words."

Lee recalls seeing Brown one night at the bar at the Harvest Café and Bakery in Oxford, where Lee and some friends often played on Tuesday nights. Brown had seen the Oxford alt-country band Blue Mountain recently, "and he instantly loved them. So he asked me to introduce him to them, which I did. I was always struck by the fact that, here was this rising author with a particularly high profile around town, who was humble enough not to feel like he could walk up to this young band and say, 'Hi, I'm Larry Brown.' He wanted a secondary introduction.

"That impressed me, and it showed his deep respect for musicians."

"You ask what makes our kind of music successful. I'll tell you. It can be explained in just one word: sincerity. When a hillbilly sings a crazy song, he feels crazy. When he sings, 'I Laid My Mother Away,' he sees her a-laying right there in the coffin. He sings more sincere than most entertainers, because the hillbilly was raised tougher than most entertainers. You got to know a lot about hard work. You got to have smelt a lot of mule manure before you can sing like a hillbilly. The people who has been raised something like the way the hillbilly has, knows what he is singing about and appreciates it. For what he is singing is the hopes, and prayers, and dreams and experiences of what some call the 'common people.' I call them the 'best people,' because they are the ones that the world is made up most of. They're really the ones who make things tick, wherever they are in this country, or in other countries. . . . There ain't nothing at all queer about them Europeans liking our kind of singing. It's liable to teach them more about what everyday Americans are really like than anything else." Hank Williams, 1953.

Sometime near the end of his life, Brown had a business card printed up that he handed out to friends and associates. Above his address and phone number it read:

LARRY BROWN
HUMAN BEING

"Are you Chip?" I ask the well-dressed bartender at The Coop, the candlelit bar on the fourth floor of our hotel. He smiles. "I am not Chip, no. I think he's around, though, hold on."

With that he leaves his post behind the bar and makes a quick stroll out onto the patio deck and back. "Nope, not here, thought he was. Sorry. Pretty sure he's working at City Grocery tomorrow night, that's where he usually is." We console ourselves by taking our beers outside on the patio and enjoying a modestly sweet view of Oxford Square. The mid-March evening is cool and pleasant, and above yellow lights and darkened storefronts and a few people in shirtsleeves strolling the sidewalks, with the Confederate Flag flying across the street in front of a municipal building, we drink.

"Are you Chip?" I ask the next night, doubtfully, to a young, clean-cut guy behind the upstairs bar at City Grocery. "Uh, nope, I'm not." I'm starting to wonder. We console ourselves by retiring to a small table against the wall, sipping one of the most wonderful bourbons we'd sipped in ages, a locally brewed spirit. Moments later, after pausing to admire Lamar Sorrento's fabulous primitivist paintings of Bo Diddley, Chuck Berry, Johnny Cash, and Hank Williams, we gaze out the large front window onto the dusky Square, and I wonder about Chip.

Earlier that day, we'd eaten lunch at Ajax Diner, enjoying catfish and fries, red beans and rice, and steamed broccoli and coleslaw, plus a couple of Larry Brown Ales, a special beer made by Yalobusha Brewing Company in Water Valley, Mississippi, in honor of Oxford's late hero. I'd heard that Brown had often taken his young family to Ajax, that their regular table was located near the back, on the right, against the wall. That section of the restaurant was closed when we were there, but the waitress kindly allowed me to search for the table. I knew I'd found the table when I spotted above it a poster for the film adaptation of *Big Bad Love*, released in 2001. As I composed a photo of the poster with my phone, a different waitress paused to let me take the snap. "Are you a fan?" she asked me. I told her yes, and why I was in town. She gazed toward the empty table and gushed, "Oh, they came in here all the time!" I thanked her and let her go back to work. I looked at the little black-table red-seat booth, smiled, and conjured a woman, a man, three kids.

"Have you seen Chip yet?" the woman behind the desk asks us hopefully when we return. We shrug apologetically.

A FEW MONTHS earlier, Jean W. Cash, who wrote *Larry Brown: A Writer's Life*, told me in an email that Larry Brown's son Shane was blogging. I'd been trying to track him down without luck, and I was grateful for her tip. I'd wanted to ask Shane if I could arrange to read and write about his father's unfinished screenplay.

By way of unseen machinations in faraway Hollywood, Brown had found himself with an opportunity that he'd never considered. One afternoon in the early 2000s, film producer Ben Myron (*Cheaper by the Dozen, One False Move*) opened his mailbox to find Brown's novel *Joe*; a friend in the music business had gifted Myron with a subscription to a monthly Southern-themed book club, which included Brown's fourth book. "That's how I first came across Larry," Myron told me. He read the novel and thoroughly loved it. His friend and associate, the actor, director, and musician Billy Bob Thornton, had been casting around for film ideas. "I gave that to Billy Bob and he thought, *Yeah, this guy's got a real voice.*" Thornton had long wanted to play Hank Williams in a bio-pic; over lunch, he and Myron agreed that they'd found the guy to write it. Thornton and Myron self-financed the screenplay and pitched the idea to Brown through his agent. "What they asked me to do," Brown said in 2003, "was take it from 1937 when [Williams] was fourteen to the first few days of '53 when he was dead and buried, and everything in between." Once terms were arranged, a contract and a commission secured, Brown agreed to write the screenplay. On January 6, 2003, he sat in front of his computer in a narrow room filled with books and CDs on the opposite side of his home's breezeway that he'd made over into his writing study, and he began to work.

He was a bit at sea. With limited experience writing screenplays, and on the hunt for inspiration, he turned to esteemed roots music writer Colin Escott, whose 1994 *Hank Williams: The Biography*, written with the assistance of

George Merritt and William MacEwen, had earned a sterling
reputation within the checkered tradition of Hank biographies.
Brown had consulted other biographical sources, but "Colin's
was the main novel. His had a whole lot of direct quotes, things
that were actually said, and I was able to go to some of those
CDs and hear exactly what was said at the mike at the Grand
Ole Opry, say, on September 22, 1951, between Red Foley and
Hank. In some cases I had to just make it up. I didn't know
what all was said between him and Lefty Frizzell or between
him and Audrey. I didn't know a lot of things that went on, so
I just had to try to make it all up for them."

Escott has been besotted with Williams since his teen years.
"I was a blues fan then, and responded to Hank as a blues
singer," he told me. In the 1980s, while working at PolyGram
Records where Williams's MGM recordings were housed,
Escott persuaded the label to release what was at the time a
complete edition of Williams's work on eight double LPs,
a high-water mark in Williams's discography. Subsequent
exchanges and conversations among collectors, industry people,
and musicians who'd known Williams sparked Escott's native
archivist instincts: *Hank's story needs to be told, respectfully
and accurately, and it needs to happen soon.* "Unlike jazz
and classical, country music was considered unworthy of
documentation during the few years that Williams was alive,"
Escott points out. "If you aggregated all the interviews with
him they'd fill less than a page. Strip away the public relations

aspect of those interviews and it amounts to very little. So his story was bound up in the memories of men and women who were, sadly but inevitably, fewer in number every year. I wanted to get the story down while I still could." He adds: "As of today, from among fifty or sixty band members, I believe just two are still living, perhaps three. And one has Alzheimer's. Hank revealed little of himself in anything but song. It wasn't the tell-all age. So it really all hinged on those who knew him and a few court documents and depositions."

Williams's brief life was particularly cinematic, Escott feels, "because it was so short and had such a natural dramatic arc. It had sex and drugs and rock and roll. It was a story of self-redemption: a man from a desperately poor background rising to the top of his profession and writing songs that are still performed." Buoyed by the biography, Brown contacted the writer and drove from Oxford to Escott's home in Hendersonville, Tennessee, to Talk Hank and listen to and marvel at the then-unissued tapes of Williams on the Mother's Best Flour Company radio shows, broadcast in the early 1950s on Nashville's WSM radio station. (The seventy-two shows, containing over 140 songs, were issued on fourteen CDs by Time Life in 2010; Escott provided the liner notes.) "They're Williams's most revealing recordings because he talks about himself and sings songs that influenced him," Escott says. "So I played those for Larry and we talked about what we'd heard and about Williams's life and art. He went outside to smoke several times. We drank a few beers. He talked about working for the fire department."

Back in Oxford, Brown hunkered down and began to obsess. Gary Hawkins remembers that "Larry got more into Hank the more he read about him. I remember his intense fascination with Hank's mother, who was a big strong woman who constantly beat up her son. Larry was fascinated with this brutal woman's effect, and he kept bringing it up." He adds: "I know Larry did a lot of research and for a while it was eating him up," and once Brown signed on to write the screenplay, "he became obsessed with Williams and the whole thing took another direction."

That direction led down a thorny road that Brown didn't particularly want to visit. A conventional screenplay runs to roughly 120 pages, or a minute or so of screen time per page; early on, Brown realized that he was in trouble. "If I only devote ten pages to each year for sixteen years, that's 160 minimum," he complained in an interview in 2003. By February of that year, the screenplay sat at 120 pages and 142 scenes, and counting; agonizingly, Brown lost those pages on his computer to a corrupt file, and he had to start over. The reset didn't temper his ambition, however, and the screenplay quickly swelled again. "I thought I was going to get it done in ninety days, so I set aside ninety days. But the ninety days went by and I wasn't halfway through." The year 2003 evolved into the Year of Hank: Brown worked on the screenplay virtually every night for eight months, between home and family duties and the odd writing assignment. "It was the most intensive period of work that I've had in a long time, including finishing *The Rabbit Factory*," he said. "I didn't work as hard on this novel as I've been working on this screenplay." Brown squeezed in a brief promotional trip to Austin, Texas, "then I had eight more days off and I told myself that I needed every one of those eight days to go and revise and everything." Brown's first draft of what he was calling "A House of Gold: The Hank Williams Story" ended up an enormous, unwieldy, wholly impractical, virtually unfilmable 584 pages. "That's what I come up with," he sighed.

The prospect of editing sometimes bothered Brown, who was an inveterate over-writer. His editor Shannon Ravel speaks of his immense manuscript drafts landing heavily on her desk at Algonquin Books, and she and Brown both admitted to enduring sometimes fiery confrontations over the inevitable edits. Fiction writer Clyde Edgerton, a longtime friend of Brown's, recalled for me a telling incident near the end of Brown's work on the screenplay:

> We're in a hotel room. I think it's in Decatur County, Georgia. It was a book thing. I'm in his room, he's on the bed. It's five o'clock, and he's got a five fifteen interview with somebody downstairs. He's lying on the bed talking, and we're talking, and as I recall he's sober. I'm

worried about his interview, but, you know, I won't say anything about it. A good buddy, Tom Rankin, and I always talk about Larry Time, very different from Normal Time. And he said, "You know, Clyde, that script is over five hundred pages long." I said, "Larry!" I thought he might be kidding a little bit. I kinda looked at him, and he was dead serious. He said, "And they want me to cut it! But Clyde, how can I take a hunk out of a man's life?"

Edgerton admits now that he felt somewhat surprised that Brown didn't have a better feel for what he was doing, "but that was one thing about Larry. He was dead serious on writing this screenplay, and dead serious that it had to be five hundred pages. He couldn't cut it because it would be detrimental to the man, detrimental to leave stuff out of his life that Larry felt had to be in there." In the hotel room, the phone rang. "I knew what it was, it was the damn interview!" Edgerton remembers, laughing. "By now it was five fifteen or whatever. He hung up the phone, got up, put on some clothes, went into the bathroom, came out. I'm looking at my watch and I'm sweating, because he's missed this fucking interview. He goes out the door, turns around and looks at me, and says, 'I hate it when they rush me.'"

Myron and Thornton wouldn't rush Brown, but neither could they pay him for a second draft. "We never got the financing together to make the movie," Myron acknowledges. "We financed the screenplay ourselves, but then to make the movie we needed someone to finance the movie and we could never get that together. I liked the screenplay a lot; I thought it was very strong. It was just, of course, way too long."

Brown's "House of Gold" *was* enormous, narrated too much of a life, took up block after block. Unwilling to work without pay, hesitant to edit anyway, Brown set aside the screenplay and devoted himself to finishing *A Miracle of Catfish*. In that novel, a young boy named Jimmy rides his beloved go-kart up and down the road in front of his family's trailer every day until dark, hoping against hope that his dad—a philandering loser who's given only "Jimmy's dad" as sobriquet—will buy him and his sisters tickets to a Kenny Chesney concert. This being a Larry Brown novel, Jimmy's dad fails to deliver. Jimmy's yearning to go see Chesney play, to commune in a happy crowd of fans, is thwarted. But Brown died before he completed the novel. Does Jimmy ever get to go and hear country music? We'll never know.

I contacted Shane Brown in October. I introduced myself and asked if he knew the whereabouts of the screenplay, as the librarians at the University of Mississippi had informed me that the manuscript wasn't in the Larry Brown collection there. I asked him if I could read the screenplay if it turned up; he copied on his mother and a close family friend to the email thread and replied that he'd hunt for it in his dad's writing room when he found the time. Two months later I received an email from him that read, "I've got good news. . . ." Later that day he sent a photo of the screenplay's cover page.

IN MARCH, AMY and I drive down from DeKalb. Shane works for a landscaping crew in Oxford and can't meet me until after five o'clock. Late afternoon on a Monday, I leave Oxford, navigating the quiet square, drive east out of town, turn south at a car-and-truck dealership, and drive a dozen or so miles on Route 334, a pleasant, winding road through dairy and beef cattle farmland dotted with churches and modest wooden and red-brick single-story homes. The Brown Dairy Farm, operated by Shane's brother Billy Ray, comprises seventy acres of hilly, green pastures, and is thriving; Billy Ray leases another fifteen hundred acres to farmers in Lafayette County. I shoot past the home several times before we finally connect; Shane helpfully waits for me at the end of his drive in a black Toyota truck—his dad's. Named for the titular character of the 1953 Western (a favorite of Brown's), Shane, who is thirty-seven and energetic, hops out of his truck, directs me to park at an angle on the front yard in front of a redbrick ranch home, and greets me. He is a virtual copy of his dad: he's of medium height, has a compact frame and a ruddy, narrow, creased face that often blossoms into a crinkly smile. His eyes are bright, and he wears a trimmed reddish-brown beard. Often during our conversations he removes his trucker's cap to run his hands though his cropped hair.

He leads me directly into a room off of the breezeway. "We keep it unlocked," he says mildly. I notice the letters *C O O L* affixed to the door, above scattered postcards. "Yeah, dad called it Cool Pad but he never got around to puttin' the other word up," Shane explains. We step into the narrow, carpeted room, maybe four feet wide and a dozen feet long, and Shane switches on an overhead light. The air's musty and a touch moldy, and he sends a ceiling fan moving. A low, cinder-block-and-wood-plank bookshelf runs along on one side, two acoustic guitars leaning against it, and on the other side shelves hold framed photographs, pottery, plate ware, an empty Bud Light can or two, and more books. Affixed to the walls like so many moths are movie posters, concert fliers, mementoes from readings and lectures Brown gave, a few framed broadsides, and dozens of photographs of family and friends and musicians, many coiling with age. On the far end of the room a black leather high-backed chair sits in front of a mid-century metal desk that barely holds a vintage turntable, amplifier, speakers, and towering stacks of CDs reaching to the ceiling. Manuscript stacks dot the room (many, I'll learn, unpublished stories and essays of Brown's). As if Brown had just pulled them off, a pair of black cowboy boots sits in repose next to the desk. On the wall, hanging from a silver string, is a shiny black Danelectro guitar with two Post-it notes affixed to the bottom, one reading, "HANK SEPT. 17 1923," the other, "DEAD JAN. 1 1953." Shane points to the guitar: "I thought of you when I saw that," he says.

After a few minutes, Shane asks me if I want to visit the writing shack that his dad built on his land in Tula, a ten-or-so-minute drive away. The sun's setting quickly, and as we climb into his truck, Shane opens the can of beer resting in his drink holder. "I'm having myself a cold one. Do you want one?" I say sure, and Shane reaches into the backseat and hands me a Bud Light. As we head along 334 and turn south onto 445, we sip our beers and Shane talks about his brother's dairy and beef cattle farm, his own semi-satisfying work as a landscaper, his family, a bit about his dad and his work and legacy. We drive into increasingly rural land, and he points out a patch of woods here, a two-bedroom trailer there, a convenience store long-gone, places where his dad had based characters and scenes in his novels.

Brown's wife's family owns seven acres of land in Tula. After turning left on a cutoff road, we arrive, drive through an open gate, park out front next to a "Trump 2016" sign, and walk around back. Rain had fallen for several days in northern Mississippi before I visited, and the ground, mostly mud anyway, is still wet. Shane lives in this cabin now, and writes some, and when he's home from work or done milking the cows at his brother's farm he likes to kick back with a few beers and play guitar, like his dad. In the backyard we walk around a darkening pond to the abutting one-room shack, which Larry Brown designed and built himself over several years after cutting back considerable high grass and brush, clearing tress, and excavating the cove. Inside, Shane shows me his dad's writing desk at a window overlooking the pond, and the homemade candelabra that descends from the ceiling and provides the only light in the room. Brown is buried on this land, and after we pay our respects at his gravestone, we stand at the pond edge, drink beer, and listen to the cicadas and bullfrogs sing startlingly loudly. The afternoon quickly grows dark.

While driving back to Yocona, the truck's headlights cutting through the dark, I ask Shane to talk about the bars that his dad drank in, which ones are still around, which are gone. He tells me about an over-enthusiastic fan at City Grocery—Larry Brown's bar of choice in his later years—who'd recently tried to pry off the plaque bearing Brown's name marking his regular stool; the bar owner intervened in time, and the plaque's now safe in the frame of a photo behind the bar. Shane also tells me how raising children and generally growing older had tempered his dad's social habits a bit, that near the end of his life he didn't escape home for the Oxford bars quite as often. I think about a comment Brown had made in 2003, when asked by a reporter about his personal demons: *I'm doing pretty good, I reckon. I just try to stay home and stay out of bars and stay out of trouble.* I ask Shane if he thinks that Hank Williams's drinking interested his dad.

"Sure, yeah, absolutely," he says quickly, one hand on the wheel, one around his Bud Light. His voice grows quieter. "Yup." He pauses. "His life, his roughness, I would say. His rowdiness."

BACK AT THE Cool Pad, Shane offers me another beer and shuts the door behind us, walks to his dad's desk, and pushes aside a stack of manuscript sheets. "Yeah, here it is," he says, and he produces an enormous three-ring binder, at least four inches thick. "You just sit there. I'm gonna hang out. I might have a friend over later."

I sit in Brown's chair at Brown's writing desk and consider the behemoth before me. "If it can be written, or thought, it can be filmed," said Stanley Kubrick, and in my mind's eye I see Brown nodding grimly. Dated September 2003, the first and only draft of "House of Gold: The Hank Williams Story" runs to 673 scenes over 584 pages. If in a conventional screenplay one pages equals approximately one minute of screen time, then Brown has written a ten-hour miniseries, or at least the most unconventional feature-film bio-pic in Hollywood history. The binder's so full it barely lays flat on the desk. Overwhelmed, I page through the screenplay, doubtful that I can absorb the draft in one sitting, or ten. To me the problem appears threefold. Brown couldn't or wouldn't rein in his writing in his early drafts. He relied overly faithfully on Escott's biography. And he didn't know how to write a screenplay.

"The thing with biographies is you want to shine a light on certain aspects of someone's life and put other aspects in the shadows," Ben Myron told me. "If you shine a light on the whole life it becomes a little bit long. It's challenging, because you have to kind of edit yourself as you're going, or you have to figure out what it is that you're gonna focus on, certain relationships, a certain period of time, a certain event, that kind of thing, and build from there." Brown, conversely—perversely—adapted Escott's thoroughly researched book rather than selected iconic moments from Williams's life, forgetting, or stubbornly refusing to acknowledge, that he wasn't writing a book but composing a story to keep moviegoers in their seats for ninety minutes or two hours.

I gaze up at the CDs towering over me: Gillian Welch, Jim Reeves, Robert Earl Keen Jr., Buddy Miller, Patty Loveless, Tim McGraw, Charley Pride, Vic Chesnutt, Ben Weaver, Blue Mountain, Wilco, Leonard Cohen, Dylan. These were only a few of Brown's kindred spirits and partners in crime, fellow artists whose music he'd play when he needed refreshing, or needed to hear something articulated that he felt but couldn't yet name, or just needed a good time or maybe to help, with the beer and the bourbon, stave off the noise coming from the cardboard box sitting on top of his stereo receiver, on which he'd scrawled in black ink, THIS BE THE BOX WHERE I PUT ALL THE SHIT—mostly, it seems, bills and business. Gazing a bit higher, I note a "Faulkner and Religion" poster from a Faulkner and Yoknapatawpha Conference at the University of Mississippi peeking over the top of a CD shelf, next to an oversized poster promoting Brown's own *Big Bad Love*.

Outside, Shane's friend has arrived, and I can hear Shane and her talking quietly and opening beers in the front yard.

I return to the screenplay. I try to digest the fact that Brown seems to have included virtually every scene in Escott's book, as he took Myron and Thornton's charge to heart: go from '37 to '53 and everything in between. (*How can you take a hunk out of a man's life?*) As far as I can tell, the historical and bio-graphical details throughout the screenplay are accurate. Early scenes are set in evocative places: a music store in Montgomery, Alabama; a radio station; Williams's mother Lillie's boarding house, where Williams lived off and on; a honky-tonk bar. For the record, Williams is declared dead at the Oak Hill Hospital in Scene 657, and his funeral, packed with mourners, takes place in Scene 669. Toby Marshall figures prominently—he's the forgery convict who, after his release from the Oklahoma State Penitentiary in 1951, met Williams and convinced him that he was a medical doctor, eventually prescribing for Williams reckless amounts of amphetamines, Seconal, chloral hydrate, and morphine. In the screenplay, Brown describes Marshall as a "small, pasty angel of death," and establishes a parallel narrative between Marshall's legal and incarceration woes and Williams's meteoric rise; their meeting is fated, and fateful. Generally, Brown captures Williams's voice and ver-nacular well: "She's gonna raise nine hunnerd hells," he has Williams moaning to a bandmate about returning home to Audrey. And he exhibits a strong feel for the mortality dog-ging Williams through his intense suffering: in a comparatively cheerful scene set at Christmas in the Williams Franklin Road house in Nashville, Brown notes "on the wall, a clock ticks away Hank's time." In the screenplay's 673rd and final scene, Williams's girlfriend Bobbie Jett gives birth to a baby girl, several days after Williams's funeral. Brown seems to have wanted to evoke something being set in motion just as something was ending.

One provocative decision Brown made was to dramatize the activities of a couple, named only Elderly Fan and Wife, who act as a kind of rural Greek chorus throughout the screenplay. I mentioned this later to Myron and he said, "Oh yeah, Larry's signature." The couple appear early in the screenplay, making their way to Williams's concerts; once, their vehicle breaks down but they're determined to get to the show. Brown seems to have viewed these older fans as essential country folk, Williams's true fans, the ones he wrote the songs for and who understood him on a simple but urgent level. (Hank: *For what he is singing is the hopes, and prayers, and dreams and experiences of what some call the 'common people.'*) Awed and respectful, the couple shows up at Williams's packed funeral, where these exchanges occur:

Elderly Fan: You reckon Hank knowed all these people?

Wife: I bet he did.

and

Wife: You know what, Paw?

Elderly Fan: What, Maw?

Wife: I wish we could've took him fishin' or somethin'. Wouldn't that have been nice?

Elderly Fan: It sure would've, Maw. I heard he loved to fish.

I don't know whether these scenes would've made it past revisions or, if they did, whether they wouldn't have reeked of sentimentality—but Brown was never too afraid to laud the modest desires and pleasures, not to mention the earnest naïveté, of his rural characters, the delight of hours of noiseless fishing, the wonder at, and the skepticism about, citified material successes. For Brown, Elderly Fan and Wife seem to be stand-ins for all of Williams's admirers who saw him as a country boy singing the truth, no matter how dark that truth got, and no matter how successful their boy got. The rumors of his drunkenness and womanizing, the no-shows? *Well, yeah, but the boy can sing.*

"So, did it end?" Shane asks when I emerge from the Cool Pad after a couple of hours. I can barely see him and his friend in the dark.

"Well, yeah," I say. "He ended it."

Amy and I return a couple of days later to pay our respects to Shane and to thank him again for his hospitality. He introduces us to his sister-in-law and other family members, the youngest of whom is riding around the farm on a pony, shirt-less, delightedly chased by other kids. Dogs run to and fro. "Lots of people, friends and family, just wander in and out of here," Shane remarks. We walk across the yard to the barn and watch him set up his elaborate cow-milking equipment before we duck in to the writing room so I can take a last look around. At Brown's desk, Amy asks, "What's this?" She points to a photo that had curled closed; I hadn't noticed it. She carefully lifts the photo with her finger. It's a sepia-toned image of Hank Williams, suited up, gazing into the camera and leaning against a car, strumming an acoustic, from the cover of *The Complete Hank Williams* ten-CD box set. She lets go of the photo, and it curls shut. We leave Oxford the next day.

"I CAN'T IMAGINE Hank Williams being all that different from Larry," Clyde Edgerton said to me. "Hank had to be serious in a way that Larry was serious, which kind of defied believability in the most beautiful way in the world. When I see Hank, those little films and stuff, there's somebody who looks kinda shy, who's just completely overcome with the notoriety that he has, not in the dark, and not unaware, but unschooled about how you might handle notoriety, positive notoriety. What do you do with that? He had no clue.

"I guess Larry was planning to cut the screenplay at some point. If he had gotten it into his head that he had to cut it back to a hundred and thirty pages, and he really believed he had to, if somebody said it's never gonna hit the screen unless you do that, I believe he would've done it."

WHO KNOWS WHAT would've been in store for Hank Williams had he lived past his twenty-ninth birthday. Some commenters feel that, like many of his country-music peers, he might've been left gasping in the wake of the Sun Records revolution in Memphis in the mid- and late 1950s. "Hank's music, like that of his contemporaries, was adult in content," observes Colin Escott in *Hank Williams: The Biography*. "Rock 'n' roll was teenage music. The exaggeration and overstatement of rock 'n' roll were alien to the fundamental values of Hank's music, and the sledgehammer beat was the opposite of The Drifting Cowboys' sweet, mellow swing." A few of Williams's records, such as "Hey, Good Lookin'" and "Settin' the Woods on Fire," "prefigured rock 'n' roll to some extent," Escott notes, "but that was no guarantee that he could have weathered the storm any better than his contemporaries. Rhythm 'n' Blues singer Wynonie Harris had much of what became the rock 'n' roll swagger on his late '40s and early '50s hits, like 'Good Rockin' Tonight,' but that didn't help him score one hit after rock 'n' roll broke. He was too old and too black. Hank was probably too old and too hillbilly. But by dying prematurely, he avoided the indignity of trying to answer the question of what he would have done. He also left the tantalizing promise of what might have been as well as a blank screen upon which vested interests could project all manner of fantasies."

A *Miracle of Catfish* suggested that Brown was continuing to evolve as a writer. Following the misstep of *The Rabbit Factory*'s somewhat labored formal experimentation, A *Miracle of Catfish* arrived a few years after Brown's death burdened with grief but fully alive. Though the novel's unfinished, the world Brown creates is so full, the characters so round and naturalistic, the rolling, tense, and verdant landscape so sensually rendered, that the lack of any conventional resolution feels more realistic than not: this world is alive and unending. Loneliness, alienation, aimless driving, splintered families, beers on ice in a cooler in a truck's floorboards, sticky heat, human anxieties and drama: Brown had explored it all before, but the interior lives of Jimmy, the young boy with the awful father, and Cortez, the old man up the road who befriends Jimmy, are more dimensional and innate than Brown had ever achieved. Had he lived, I only wonder what worlds, and what forsaken but proud and determined men, women, and children in them, Brown might've imagined for us on the winding roads and off-roads of his beloved, beleaguered northern Mississippi.

I NEVER DID track down Chip, friend of Larry's, local bartender extraordinaire. That made a kind of sense, finally. Spirits abounded on this trip. When I sat at Larry Brown's writing

desk, I imagined him ghosting the same chair, fresh out of his
boots maybe, a beer open, a cigarette lit, a manuscript hot in
front of him. I imagined the CDs he'd take with him when he
needed a break, wanted to go ride into the gloam in the truck
that I'd sat in, on the roads I'd been on with his son. Brown
had been chasing Hank Williams, hoping that Hank might stop
long enough somewhere between the reality and the myth so
that Brown could get a good, long look, maybe to get inside the
man who sang such brutally simple songs about brutally complex things like love, loss, and heartache. I don't know what
dimensions Larry Brown's "House of Gold" would've ended up
assuming, whether Brown would have knocked out a floor or
the attic, or reduced it to rubble and made it all over again—he
did build houses, after all, and if he was paid for it, he sure as
hell would try—or whether he ever could've allowed himself to
reduce a man like that.

I WOULD HAVE HAD TO HAVE
BEEN A DIFFERENT PERSON
TO LISTEN TO HÜSKER DÜ

AELSTROM NOT BEING my modus operandi in the 1980s, raised as I was on the Monkees and the "Red" and "Blue" albums, tuned as I was to the Beatlesesque, to hooks-per-minute, to the T.A.M.I. Show, R&B, to Weasel on WHFS 102.3 FM carrying the torch of 1960s AM radio into the alternative decade, noise being for me something I knew all too well internally as a kind of obsessive litany of voices, of personas watching me watching me watch myself, seeking instead through rock and roll a way to lift myself out of my lousy self, a self insisting on analysis and overthinking, seeking in rock and roll grins and self-mockery and good times against the earnestness I heard in hardcore and post-hardcore, and let's face it, the fear I felt in the scowling face of that music, chagrined to this day that I turned down an invitation from the quiet girl who lived above the "Zoo bar" on Connecticut Avenue to see the Dead Kennedys, turned her down out of silliness, couldn't let go, because as a punk she scared me, not as a "punk," but as a woman who was willing to hear more than I was in noise and in formlessness, who stood a few feet closer to chaos, admitting to darkness that I indulged in in the books I read and the movies I watched and the bad poetry I wrote, but darkness that I avoided in amplification, preferring Mod to Rocker, skinny tie to Doc Marten boots, the Slickee Boys to Minor Threat, and so I avoided the roar, and when I listen to Hüsker Dü now and regret what I missed—*Zen Arcade* and *New Day Rising*, the transcendent shows, the camaraderie among folks who in my puniness unnerved me—I know that I would have had to have been a different person then, a kid willing to fall into the limitless darkness of a mouth roaring, letting go of pop songs and formalism, of mid-1960s hooks and riffs and their modest, three-button suit revolts; I would have had to have let go, and when I did and went to see Hüsker Dü at the Psychedelly in Bethesda in 1984, my fears were founded, though played off coolly, as I stood as near as I would have ever let myself to the roar, the loudest show I'd seen, loud in *Yes* to the anarchic and disorder as well as pure wattage and sound, as Mould and Grant stomped and screamed and required that I look where they were looking, too, my ears ringing and my face red, and when the kid jumped up onstage to sing along to a song and forgot the words and stood next to Mould looking like a lost kid, humiliated, the complicated look on his face was a relief to me, something human, something behind a pose, a kindness, actually, betrothed me from somewhere, so that if I had let go and gone down into the frightening roar this kid and I might've shared a moment of understanding, or vulnerability, something, had I let go.

MAMA LOVED THE WAYS OF THE WORLD

You're ruining your reputation
and I can give you two big reasons why

—"PLEASE DON'T GO TOPLESS, MOTHER,"
AS SUNG BY SEVEN-YEAR-OLD TROY HESS

*I*N THE CANNON of country music there are countless odes to broken hearts, depraved dalliances, and
dark taverns, but precious few numbers about go-go dancers
and the men who gawk at them. Consider the road toward or
away from redemption walked by the man trailing hot pants
and knee-high boots, his ageless conflicts between the secular
and the sacred, his wallet and his God, his dancer and his wife.
Nashville songwriter Harlan Howard defined a triumphant
country record as "Three chords and the truth"; I'm surprised
that more Music City songwriters don't pen odes to the truths
embodied in scantily dressed women who move in and out of
bright lights. Bump and grind, high heels, and a downcast gaze:

a lurid imagination easily admits both the nude dancer and the man in the Nudie suit staring up at her. Yet the tradition of country and roots music about go-go dancers is, well, skimpy.

For years, record collector and WFMU disc jockey Greg Germani has searched hills and hollers for country songs about exotic dancing, for that "improbably cultural collision between Nashville or, if not Nashville proper, somebody doing his best to emulate the Nashville approach in many cases, and the rapidly changing social culture of the times." Germani adds, "It's the same weird vibe that comes through on the country records that address hippies, miniskirts, hot pants, and marijuana." At such "a disjointed intersection of very different worlds," Germani indulges the rare opportunity to hear semi-sleazy lyrics about go-go dancers or strippers. "It's very appealing when those lyrics are embedded within the context of a country record," he notes, "coming as it does from a place that's usually more tradition bound." On WFMU's *Rock & Soul Ichiban* blog, Germani (as "Greg G") and his like-minded cohorts post MP3s of country go-go records, oddball 45s found in used bins, thrift stores, and record fairs, including Bernie Waldon's "Bright Lights and Go-Go Girls," the Great Pretender's "Really Big Country Go-Go Shew," Sally Marcum's "Go-Go Girls," Leona Williams's "Country Girl With the Hot Pants On," Bobby Jenkins's "If You Ain't Gonna Take It Off (Don't Tempt Me Baby)," and Don Hagen's "Bright Lights A Go-Go" and "I'm Gonna See the Go-Go Girls Tonight."

My favorite might be "Daddy Was a Preacher but Mama Was a Go-Go Girl," recorded in the early 1970s by, among others, Betty Jo Bangs and Jo Anna Neel. Neel's peppy, horn-driven recording—produced by Joe Johnson and released as a single on Decca Records in 1971—is in my opinion the best. Emerging as it did from a tradition that's barely there, "Daddy Was a Preacher but Mama Was a Go-Go Girl" is a campy curio. The narrative unfolds in the song's title: a woman sings about the "craziest love happening anywhere," an improbable marriage between her preacher daddy and her go-go-dancing mama. "Daddy loved the bible, but mama loved the ways of the world," the daughter sings as planets collide, and, though "people used to stare at the oddest couple anywhere . . . my daddy didn't see her through the eyes of the world." The words are gaily sung, and there's nothing too aggressive or untoward in the musicians' playing, nothing in the vocals that hints at the myriad tensions that might be shared by a man of the cloth and his go-go-dancing wife. The story is offered up as a joke, a winking, can-ya-believe-this-world tale pitched at those among the country establishment made uncomfortable by rising hem lines and the general plummeting of moral standards in the era of bra burning and *Ms.* magazine. *Just look how cute that crazy couple is!*

Some cultural encoding must have been going on here. A God-fearing preacher in a country song is recognizable, a tasseled go-go dancer less so, and I wonder if she's identified by her

Hullabaloo silhouette rather than a stripper pole because strip tease was too risqué for even the rapidly evolving 1970s. The Neels were likely bowing to decorum, with their audience—and their radio programmers—in mind. Imagining a preacher married to and enduring the sitcom antics of a frosty-lipped extra from an Elvis movie must have been easier than imagining him in a marriage bed with a hussy who takes it all off. It was the early '70s and cultural change was in the air, but in myriad ways country music looks backward more often than it looks ahead.

Each singer who recorded "Daddy Was a Preacher but Mama Was a Go-Go Girl" tweaked the lyrics slightly. Betty Jo Bangs arrives at one of my favorite couplets in pop music:

> They'd say, Papa would preach fire and brimstone,
> Mama did The Monkey in her cage all alone.

There's some conflict for you.

I WAS INTRODUCED to "Daddy Was a Preacher but Mama Was a Go-Go Girl" in the early '90s at a show at the Union Bar and Grill in Athens, Ohio, by the riotous North Carolina band Southern Culture on the Skids. Between staging a sweaty limbo dancing contest on the floor and tossing fried chicken wings into the crowd, the band dove into a high-energy version of the tune, smiling bassist Mary Huff belting out the number through bee-stung lips beneath her beehive hairdo. Southern Culture's rocking version is a blast—it appears on their 1992 album *For Lovers Only*—and the lone concession to the years since the original song's appearance is the louder, amped-up arrangement featuring Huff's grinning, twangy delivery and Rick Miller's peerless, echo-laden guitar picking. Southern Culture plays the song as a sly joke, too. Filtered down the decades, it arrives to us in the twenty-first century as a relic from an era wrestling with impropriety and figuring out just what's the funniest, gentlest way to send it up.

Another country song from this era originated as a joke, but from its anti-art beginnings it's morphed into a cult classic that invites incredulity more than laughter. In 1972, Ron Hellard was a nascent songwriter toiling on Music Row in Nashville, standing in the proverbial long line hoping to land the next big hit that would vault his song onto the radio, and perhaps get it warbled at the Grand Ole Opry. Hellard worked for Acoustic Music, a publishing company co-owned by Buddy Lee of Buddy Lee Attractions, where Dorothy Hess worked as a secretary. Dorothy's husband was Bennie Hess, a large, gregarious transplant from Texas with a unique, distinguished history in the country-music recording industry. His father, Vestral, had worked on the railroad in the 1920s with the "Singing Brakeman" Jimmie Rodgers, who would often stay at the Hess household. Allegedly, Rodgers taught a young Bennie how to play the guitar, and Rodgers's widow later gave Bennie one of Rodgers's instruments. (Judging by the serial number, this was one of the first Martin Guitars ever made.) Hess left school at fourteen, rode the trains and hitchhiked to California and back, eventually forming the Rhythm Wranglers among other outfits. A long career as a performer and producer followed: Hess recorded for Mercury Records, appeared on *The Louisiana Hayride* with Hank Williams, and produced Kenny Rogers's first single. Hess's work took him from the West Coast to Texas to Tennessee, where he eventually settled in Nashville in a modest home on Seventeenth Street and formed two record labels, Spade Records and Showland. On the latter he issued primarily his own releases (Hess's best-known song is "Wild Hog Hop," cut in 1958) and also several featuring his young son, Troy. Hess was casting for material for Troy when his wife Dorothy approached Hellard.

"Dorothy asked if I would write a song for her son," Hellard told me. "Troy was very young. An infant, an embryo. Anyway, I sat down right at the time she asked me, and maybe in ten minutes or so I came up with a novelty tune. Slapped it on a cassette and gave it to her right then. And that was the end of it for me. I had nothing further to do with that record." What Hellard bemusedly calls "a parody of country music" would take on a life of its own.

TROY HESS FIRST played guitar at the age of two, sang in public with Bob Wills & His Texas Playboys and released his first single ("The Ballad of Troy Hess") at the age of three, and wrote his first song when he was four. Born in 1965 and raised in Music City, USA, Troy was exposed to country musicians and their culture at a very early age, soaking up Music Row filtered through his dad's long tenure in the business. Eager to promote their young son and cash in on his early regional successes, Bennie and Dorothy were keen to listen to this "custom job" that Hellard had worked up for Troy, who was seven years old at the time. "When Hellard originally got it to my mom, she thought that it was just a joke," Troy told me. "She thought, *Aw, no way.* She knew that Hellard was an up-and-coming songwriter, but she said, 'Oh no, my son's not gonna record anything like that!'"

What Hellard had presented to Dorothy was a ditty titled "Please Don't Go Topless, Mother," a young son's desperate, half-sung, half-spoken request that his mother forego her shameful job of stripping. "I have kind of a bizarre, creative bone, I guess," Hellard says. "It just popped into my head. It didn't come from anywhere, there wasn't any thought given to it at all. Titles come to me, and that's what happened here." He adds with a chuckle, "It was *not* autobiographical."

> Mother dear, I know you must work
> though the job you got is really not the answer.
> I'm so ashamed to be the only guy in my gang
> whose mother is a topless go-go dancer.

Oh, please don't go topless, Mother.
I hate to be quite so blunt.
The kids all laugh but I don't cry
You're not the only one who's putting up a front.

Oh, please don't go topless, Mother
But I just cannot tell a lie.
You're ruining your reputation
and I can give you two big reasons why.

Please don't go topless, Mother.
Even though it buys me clothes to wear
I'd rather wear old rags, Mother.
You've got a burden you shouldn't have to bear.

[spoken]

Oh, please don't go topless, Mother.
Little friends won't come to see me (but their
Daddies do).
I'll shine shoes, I'll collect pop bottles, anything
to help out.
Then we'll go off together and start over
with no shame for the people to talk about.

The stately, somewhat stiff waltz begins at the border of
Hank Williams and Generic, strummed acoustic and electric
guitars vying for emotional bedrock, a thumped drum modestly

keeping time. The chord changes are conventional, the sound lo-fi, homespun. A voice enters. You know it's a child's, and you hear the lip-pursed clench in the pronunciation at the end of the words *answer* and *dancer* and so you know it's a Southern child's voice, his melodic uptick on the words *front* and *bear* a nice touch, plaintive. Genuine? It's hard to tell. What does the kid singer know? Does he really understand the burden about which he sings, that his mother's naked shame buys him his clothes, the complications at that intersection? He probably doesn't get the *Playboy*-napkin-era joke, "I can give you two big reasons why." After a pedestrian instrumental passage, a tinkling piano heralds the song's second half, where the boy's spoken-word section is, if not emotionally genuine, at least well-timed. Melodramatically, he dreams of running off with his mother and starting anew, before, as the song resolves, he repeats his confession that she's not the only one who's hiding from dishonor.

BENNIE AND DOROTHY Hess didn't quite know what to make of this eccentric number. "The music industry was very close in Nashville at that time," Troy remembers. "They would kick you until you got down, but by God when you got down they'd do everything they could to get you back up. So the song got around pretty quick, and pretty soon people said, 'Hey, man, you gotta get Troy to record that.' And mom said, 'No, no, no.'" Bennie and Dorothy Hess were culturally and religiously conservative, and yet they sniffed commerce in the air. "Mom and dad were both Southern Baptists. They never smoked; they never drank. No way was that song gonna fly. But finally—I think it was more my dad than my mom, because my dad was obviously a very colorful character—they thought it was a good novelty song. So he finally caved and thought, *Okay, we're gonna do it*." Bennie and Dorothy kept the title hidden from little Troy for a while before they let him look at it. "So I learned the song, and we went in to record it. I didn't even really know what 'topless' was." The phrasing, Troy remembers, came fairly natural. "This little kid is really sincere and he doesn't want her to work, doesn't want her to have to be stripping."

Says Ron Hellard now: "I assume it was a serious reading of the lyric, which should have been a lot more tongue-in-cheek for somebody to do. It's like he's singing it for real. Of course, a kid doesn't know tongue from cheek. But I was surprised by his reading on it, and maybe that has something to do with it, I don't know. Today it's pretty mild, the subject matter.

"There aren't that many country songs about strippers," he acknowledges. "It just popped into my head and I wrote it down. I thought it'd be a fun thing for a little kid to sing. I probably wouldn't have written it if I thought it'd have any kind of life to it at all."

"Please Don't Go Topless, Mother" has indeed led a curious, dogged life, a remarkable fate considering that the song was

nearly sidelined in its early days. Bennie Hess produced and promoted several independent Nashville artists as a full-time job,
and he would duly send his artists' records, including his boy's
new 45, to radio stations throughout the South. "And man, we
got that record sent back to us," Troy recalls. "We got some
nasty letters from program directors saying, 'We're not gonna
play trash like this.' Oh man, we shut down the presses on
those things." At regional DJ conventions where records were
distributed and vigorously promoted—glossy photos, 45s and
LPs stacked high on tables—"Please Don't Go Topless, Mother"
vanished quickly. Within months of its release, the 45 was difficult to find. "Once we got such bad flack, man, they pulled them
out in a heartbeat," Troy recalls. "And that was the end of it."

Yet in the parallel universe of tenacious record archivists
and reissues, it's never the end of it. Pressed in a modest run of
750 or so copies, its distribution strangled at the source, "Please
Don't Go Topless, Mother" managed to survive down the
decades as bizarre rumor and in spirited conversations among
hardcore country fans and record collectors. In 1995, the song
showed up on *God Less America*, a compilation album released
on the venerable Crypt Records label gathering "Country &
Western fer all ye Sinners 'n' Sufferers." (Featuring rare songs
including Ramblin' Red Bailey's "8 Weeks in a Barroom,"
Arkey Blue & the Blue Cowboys' "Too Many Pills," and Hi Fi
Guys' "Rock & Roll Killed My Mother," *God Less America* is
a highly recommended document of twisted, profane country

oddball-ness.) Around ten years ago, Hess was shocked when a friend called him and told him about this "trailer trash" compilation album and the song's reappearance from the dead. Its cult status virtually guaranteed, "Please Don't Go Topless, Mother" made the inevitable leap into the digital domain and the boundless world of the Internet, where it's now a staple on YouTube.

For Hess, this was not a welcome development. "That song was one of those things that I really, really, really, really, really kept under wraps," Troy admits. In the summer of 1977, when Troy was thirteen, his family moved from Nashville to Houston, Texas. Burdened with puberty and the difficulties of fitting in with a new group of school kids, the reappearance of "Please Don't Go Topless, Mother" was the last thing Troy wanted.

Some undesirable notoriety had already visited the Hess household in August of 1975 via an issue of *Country Music* magazine and its lurid headline, "Troy Hess: A Child on the Streets of Nashville." As Troy tells it, his parents had given full access to writer Mary Sue Price, who in turn neglected to run her article by them before publication. "Poor Troy Hess: The Sad Case of 'America's Singing Souvenir'" features photos of ten-year-old Troy decked out in his C&W finest, happily singing and strumming an acoustic guitar near a wishing well. In another photo, he's duetting with his father on the front porch—where a sign reads, "Troy Hess Home Office"—while his sister skips rope nearby. The article begins:

> Tonight in Nashville little Troy Hess is going downtown
> to play for the drunks on Broadway. He is going down-
> town in his red, white, and blue van seated between his
> father, a forgotten country music singer from the '30s,
> and his mother, a tiny woman with wide eyes and a sag-
> ging stomach. Troy is ten years old and tired.

Price makes no apology for the Troy Hess she witnessed, or at least for the Troy she wants to present: used by his parents, overworked, already a has-been. "Troy had cut a lot of records," Price writes, "but only one Nashville record store stocks them, and, the manager says, 'we sell one or two every now and then.' On the records, Troy's clear voice suffers from mundane arrangements and sloppy production. They sound like home tape recordings made by proud parents who hope their son might be famous someday." Price charitably quotes Bennie about the history of his son's recording career, before describing Troy playing for tourists and hustling his records on a sightseeing bus that stops in front of the Hess home. ("Nobody bought albums on the bus I rode," she notes.) Price insists that while Troy "is a charming child who loves music, enjoys show business, and adores cowboys," he's a kid who's being improperly handled by overbearing parents:

> But others have a darker view of Troy's situation.
> "It's really sad that Troy grew up," said a clerk in a

downtown Nashville record store. "The novelty of his act has worn off, but his parents keep on pushing him. Troy's father never made it as a country musician, so I guess Troy is going to have to make it. That's a big price for Troy to pay. Too big."

THE HESS FAMILY sued *Country Music* and Price for slander and for willfully misrepresenting Troy's emotional and physical conditions as well as Bennie's professional history. (Around this time the Hess family also brought litigation against PBS for airing a documentary about Outlaw Country singer David Allen Coe who'd made claims that Bennie Hess was "prostituting" his young son. Troy laments: "Suing PBS was like suing God. It was a waste of time.")

Maybe Troy just wanted to live like a normal kid. "I'd rather any day of the week be back in Texas," he tells Price in the *Country Music* article. "I'd go out in the woods and I go out in the mornin' and I don't come back till time to eat. Just spend my hours in the woods." When Troy and his family moved to Houston within a year of Price's article, Troy felt a burden that was hard to name. At home one day he turned to his mom. "I wish we hadn't recorded that song," he said to her. She assured him that that song had nothing to do with the lawsuits.

A wiser Troy felt differently: "At eleven, I knew what a topless go-go dancer was."

Troy takes umbrage at the notion that his parents treated him unfairly. "My parents never forced me to do anything," he insists. "They helped me, because obviously as a child you're not going to get anywhere without someone behind you, supporting. They bought my show clothes and paid for my records, but not one time did they force me, no one was holding a gun to my head saying, *Sing this song.* If you listen to 'Please Don't Go Topless, Mother,' does it sound like a kid in distress? No. I was just having fun with it. It was a kid singing a song."

The years following the 45's release were difficult for Troy. "With all the stuff I had dealt with, honest to God I was ready to leave all that behind. Nashville is the capital of country music, and it's pushed down people's throats so much that the kids that were in school with me at the time *hated* country music. You couldn't find a kid who claimed he liked Conway Twitty for nothing. They hated it because it was in their city every year, the different fan fairs and different conventions and stuff. They just hated it."

A telling incident occurred one afternoon at Troy's grade school, soon after the Hesses moved back to Texas. "We had a long Dodge van that my dad bought brand-new in 1972 and had customized, elongated with extra seats," Troy remembers. The white van was emblazoned with a large blue stripe that said *Troy Hess*, but by 1978 the letters were fading. "Mom let my sisters out at their school and then she pulled up to my school to let me out. I came out the side door, and there were a bunch

of these kids I'll call 'kickers,' for lack of any other term, hanging out before school. One of them yelled out, 'Well, if it ain't
the Nashville Kid!' I felt my heart sink to the floor. And in my
ignorance of myself I thought, *My God, how do they know?* I
was shocked. *Who told them?* I wanted to leave that behind.
And I shut the door and looked on the passenger side, and on
the side door my dad had written, in smaller letters, 'Showay
Productions, 820 18th Avenue South, Nashville, Tennessee,
37203, (615) 256-6351.'

"When I saw that, I realized, *Oh crap, they just saw that on
the side of the doors, no big deal.* I just tried to blend in."

FOLLOWING BENNIE HESS'S death in 1984, Troy began
looking through scrapbooks, marveling at photos of his dad
with Patsy Cline, George Jones, and other artists and industry
people he associated with over his long career. "I rediscovered
that music and realized, you know, it's not all that bad," Troy
says. "Honestly, I didn't have an appreciation for what I had.
It didn't mean anything to me. It was only after the death of
my dad that I really started growing an appreciation for what
all I'd been involved in. 'Please Don't Go Topless, Mother'
was one of those songs that I would never have played, let
anyone listen to. I've got several copies of the record, but I
never would have tried to push it, let anyone hear it before it
came out on *God Less America*. But it's one of those things
were you go, *Hey, at least they spelled your name right.* And

you need to embrace it. It is was it is. I did it. I can't go back and stop it anyway, so you just have to accept it and go on from there."

A few years ago at home in Texas, Troy received a phone call with a caller ID he didn't recognize. He picked up and soon was speaking with a woman from Los Angeles who worked for Jimmy Kimmel. One of Kimmel's writers had happened upon "Please Don't Go Topless, Mother" online and, like so many before, was wildly intrigued by the song's strangeness, unable to figure out whether it was a joke or a sincere plea. Would Troy appear on *Jimmy Kimmel Live!* and sing the song? Only, Troy insisted, if he'd also be allowed to sing a new song that he'd written. Kimmel's person assured Troy that she'd run the idea past Jimmy and his staff. The Kimmel office never called back.

RON HELLARD LEFT his novelty tune behind many years ago, enjoying a lucrative, four-decade career in Nashville. He's received multiple BMI and NSAI (Nashville Songwriters Association International) awards and has had his songs recorded by icons of country music including George Jones, Loretta Lynn, Lee Greenwood, Jerry Lee Lewis, Keith Whitley, Hank Williams Jr., Tammy Wynette, Toby Keith, and Conway Twitty. "Please Don't Go Topless, Mother," composed in minutes, will bear his name forever.

Hellard's nearly forgotten parody of country music was conceived as a joke, and as such makes barest of contact with the actual complications of sexuality, and in "Daddy Was a Preacher but Mama Was a Go-Go Girl," Jo Anna and Bob Neel sing about a crazy marriage without examining the real complexities embodied in the relationship. Such was the decorum required of a conventional country song, what Greg Germani calls "the Nashville approach" that measures the irrational in the rational structure of verse-bridge-chorus, with lyrical tropes that feel as familiar and as comforting as a pair of old cowboy boots. A preacher married to a go-go girl: all jokes aside, imagine the 3 a.m. bouts of conscience for both parties, the sexual tensions, the warring between good and evil, the triumphs of the heart, the titillating early, forbidden flirting giving way to reality, the Bible versus the Ways of the World. Think of the public censures that the preacher endures, or the skeptical snorting that the dancer overhears. Imagine the very real emotional, spiritual, and psychological complex created by opposites. And the man or woman who isn't strong enough to be an outcast, what are their options? Denial? Abnegation? Violence? None of this is really evoked in the Neels' version, which with a wink and a shimmy skirts the issues.

A certain strain of Americana songwriting of the last couple of decades originated in the personal singer-songwriter movements of the 1970s filtered through punk, post-punk, and indie candor. Products of progressive FM radio and the general cultural shift toward the confessional, songwriters like Patterson Hood who came of age in the late 1970s draw from sources as disparate as Merle Haggard, Bruce Springsteen, Neil Young, and the Rolling Stones. Hood's band is Drive-By Truckers; a pair of go-go boots stands tall and proud but lethal in the Truckers' 2011 album *Go-Go Boots*. Hood, born and raised in Alabama (his father, David Hood, was longtime bassist for the Muscle Shoals Rhythm Section), has long been interested in the tradition of Southern murder ballads and the sinister stories that they tell. "Go-Go Boots" is a slow burn that crawls menacingly as it lays out the tale of a murderous preacher and his mistress who keeps go-go boots under her bed:

> He packed a big-ass church out near Rogersville
> He drove the Cadillac, she drove the Oldsmobile
> Every Friday he shacked up with his mistress
> Doing things that he'd never do with the Mrs.
> Who was back at home cooking dinner for him. . . .
> Daddy's been preaching the word ever since he was twelve
> All about a merciful savior and the fires of hell
> I know he meant it, so what's a little straying
> He got everybody singing and a praying
> "That devil better not come back down here again"
>
> Missy wore them go-go boots; it did something for him
> Made him think his wife back home was homely and boring
> Alas, his wife back home is not long for this world.

"I wrote a trilogy of preacher murder ballads based on two actual events," Hood told me. "'The Wig He Made Her Wear' [from the Drive-By Truckers' 2010 album *The Big To-Do*] was based on the murder of a preacher in Selmer, Tennessee, by his wife, who alleged that she was moved to murder by his making her dress up like a whore, a sort of *Super Fly*–looking whore, no less, and perform wild sex with him. 'The Fireplace Poker' [from *Go-Go Boots*] is based on a different murder, this one across the river in Tuscumbia, Alabama, where a preacher had his wife killed." Later it was revealed that the preacher had likely murdered a previous wife, who had died under mysterious circumstances. When the preacher later died it was ruled a suicide, but, according to Hood, "many townsfolk think he was killed by a relative, possibly his son."

A few years later, Hood wrote "Go-Go Boots" about the same crime, "although I changed some things around. Growing up in a Bible Belt small town, there was no shortage of times when morality was shoved down our throats by people claiming to be speaking of God's will, and often they themselves were a rather shitty bunch. I spent most of my songs on *Go-Go Boots* dealing with people's quests for redemption and satisfaction in both positive and bad ways, with those two songs being of the latter." As Hood envisions her, the preacher's mistress doesn't dance for men. "To actually see exotic dancers in my hometown, you had to drive at least an hour or two to one of them bigger cities, or The Boobie Bungalow—real name—on I-65 at the Tennessee–Alabama state line."

I see those go-go boots under her bed, in the shadows, emblematic of the long, fraught journey along a woman's legs that a desperate man might take, find, or lose himself in. "I'd like to think the preacher dressed her up like an exotic dancer," Hood reflects. Imagine that. This darker place isn't an option that the dancer in "Daddy Was a Preacher but Mama Was a Go-Go Girl" has to face, headed as she is to her brightly lit home and her faithful, accepting preacher husband. Her go-go boots lay safely, demurely tucked away in the closet. I imagine that she boxes them up until she's ready again to swing and sway.

LEARNING EMPATHY
WITH SINATRA

O N A SHUTTLE bus from my downtown hotel to LAX, the driver tunes to a satellite radio station playing all Frank Sinatra. "It Happens Every Spring" comes on, a 1949 Columbia Records B-side that Sinatra recorded with the Ken Lane Quintet, a relatively obscure tune, one I've never heard, anyway. I'm travel-tired, a little hungover, and my defenses are low; I am leaving behind the balm and beauty of L.A., and the song, unbidden, slays me. In his sentimental cataloguing of springtime rituals—the new, fresh green, an older sister getting dramatic, her younger brother becoming a home-run king, Dad rolling up his sleeves to clean the attic—Sinatra brings me right back to my dad, and the three of us mingle in affection, maleness, warmth, mild embarrassment. The drive from the hotel to the airport takes roughly forty-five minutes, and the litany of prime Sinatra songs graphically affects the collective mood of the eight of us in that van, where we listen, each of us in his and her own emotional place, each with family ties strengthened or

loosened over time, to the songs that, in their outdated clas-
sicism and formal beauties, provided a soundtrack that feels
both old-fashioned and eternal. No one says a word for the
entire ride.

MY DAD IS a tremendous Sinatra fan, and I happily grew up
in a home where his records were played often. Some of my ear-
liest music memories involve listening to, and loving, the great
songs on my dad's albums: *In the Wee Small Hours*, *Songs for
Swingin' Lovers!* and especially *Sinatra's Swingin' Session!!!*
The latter's "When You're Smiling," "I Concentrate on You,"
and "My Blue Heaven" are spirited and swift, and I'd love
when, upstairs doing my homework or idling on a weekend,
I'd hear the needle drop on the family stereo in the rec room.
I knew my dad was in a good mood, and I knew that the next
hour or so was going to be fun. Sometimes, usually after dinner,
usually after a martini or two, he'd disappear down to the rec
room and in the dark listen with the headphones on, moaning
along atonally, his eyes shut. My mom would smile behind her
hands and this would become a house sound—sonorous but
wailing, tuneless but urgent—that the family would laugh at,
and about. But I intuited vaguely that those moments were nec-
essary for my dad, that somehow they were unavoidable.

I loved listening to those albums with my dad because we'd
move close together during those hours. He's of southern-
Italian heritage and it never takes much—small family joys, a

hello or goodbye hug in the front hall, a run-scoring double—to moisten his eyes. But nothing brought out his warmth and emotional life more for me than Sinatra's voice. I'd sit on the couch and listen along, and imagine my dad's younger self, that half-shadowed Brooklyn figure, Pre-Mom, more heavily accented, thinner, smiling at young women on the street whose faces I couldn't imagine, taking the subway into New York for a nickel or a dime and humming along to songs in his head.

One of his favorite Sinatra albums is the sublime *Francis Albert Sinatra & Antonio Carlos Jobim*. Pushing forty with five children, my dad bought the record when it was released in 1967. The Sinatra and Jobim collaboration created an unusual sound relative to Sinatra's earlier hard swing albums, and when it would come on I knew that my dad's mood was subtly different from when he'd play "S'posin" or "I've Got You Under My Skin," or even "Blue Moon," smiling along, shuffling his feet on the rec room floor and gently clapping his hands in the Latin mood. The Jobim album is lush, mysterious, nearly tropical in its emotional humidity; yet for all of its smoky sensuality, it's also cool, controlled, elegant. A formative album for me (with my dad's blessing I took it when I moved to graduate school), the Sinatra-Jobim partnership is of its Pop Brazilian–scented era and also, in its subtle orchestration and Claus Ogerman's nimble, elegant arrangements, utterly transcendent.

Listening to the bossa nova take on Irving Berlin's "Change Partners," I'm brought back to the 1970s and our split-level suburban home, the air-conditioned room, the period furniture, the stereo and quadraphonic speakers, my swaying dad. Is this a Saturday night and my parents home from their weekly dinner out, my dad loosened and sentimental with wine . . . ?

"THE LYRICS, JOE, the words. Listen to how he sings them." *Must you dance every dance with the same fortunate man? . . . Your lips touching his face . . . Can't you see I'm longing to be in his place?* "The way he sings them. Somehow he lets you know exactly what he's thinking. Oh. Sinatra was a master."

My dad's eyes are wet, and I'm glimpsing his romantic (romanticized?) past again, entanglements from decades earlier that I can only guess at, but his mood is weighted with something, isn't flimsily mawkish. *You know exactly what he's thinking.* What is my dad thinking: what if or what is? Sinatra's fifteen years older than my dad, singing about a heartbroken guy in a club who's contemplating a silly ruse with a hoax phone call so that he can get his shot at the girl on the dance floor. On the outside, I'm a kid. I get it. "It's his phrasing." The strings playing minor notes. I want to say, *Yeah, I hear it.*

A few days later, I gush at my dad about the final movement of George Gershwin's "Rhapsody in Blue," to which I've been listening obsessively. "Dad, I picture a guy and a girl on top of different apartment buildings in New York, looking out across the alley or the street at each other during a rainstorm, but they can't have each other!" My voice cracks. My dad gets it. I'm feverish and slightly embarrassing in my adolescent discovery, gushing. I'm returning the favor. *I know exactly what you're thinking.*

BUT FOR PERSPECTIVE: I'm butting up against my teen years, and my parents are home from their Saturday night dinner, tipsy. In our Kiss fandom, my younger brother Paul and I are listening to Paul Stanley's solo album. The four connecting Kiss solo-album posters hang on the wall in the basement, and up in the rec room we're completing the shallow pop myth. My mom and dad come downstairs, their smiles loose, their eyes a little glassy. They mutter something and laugh quietly and look at each other and start slow-dancing to Stanley's chintzy, unbearable "Tonight You Belong to Me." My brother and I are mortified, unable to know what to do, so we look at each other, and then at our feet. My parents dance in a small private circle to the corny ballad, and I flush and grow annoyed, discomfited by their tenderness.

As we've grown over the decades, my dad and I have moved closer to each other, and further away, and then close again inside the well-worn boundary of family. A regular rendezvous point for us is the bedrock humanity of Sinatra. My parents could've been swaying lovers, their romance turning on an imagined dance floor in a crowded nightclub. If I'd seen my parents not as my parents in our suburban rec room but as figures in a Sinatra ballad, I might've intuited them as grownups in love. I might've been able to more generously see my own parents, there, spotlighted, revolving into characters, characters into silhouettes, silhouettes into sound, sound into story. But that comes later.

ORIGIN STORIES

I SLEPT IN THE same bed with my younger brother until I was ten, and he was seven—at night when I had trouble sleeping he taught me to "rock," to lie on one side, fold my bottom arm beneath me, and roll gently back and forth back and forth until I got light-headed with sleepiness. Sometimes we'd do it in tandem, sometimes I'd feel him on the opposite side of the narrow bed while I was half asleep, the room dark and his silhouette moving soundlessly back and forth. Other times we'd both be up and hear the TV downstairs or our older brothers talking in the kitchen or the bedroom next door, and we'd pretend that the bed was a raft lost at sea, pitching and reeling in an ink-black storm—precisely where, in what ocean, off of what coast, we didn't pretend, it was more scary if we felt without naming it that the bed was so far from any coast as to be undiscoverable, tossed away, forgotten, and we'd shiver with chills and manufactured giggles, but I knew that we'd soon fall asleep and that the nightmare of the dark, gaping ocean would blessedly recede, and that tomorrow we'd wake up and turn on the radio and that season's hit—the Eagles' "Best of

My Love" or Eric Carmen's "All By Myself" or Captain &
Tennille's "Love Will Keep Us Together"—would pour into a
sunny room, and the forbidding ocean, not yet plaguing my
dreams as it will in the future, is nothing but a sky-blue, yellow-
tinted playground in Thor Heyerdahl's *Kon-Tiki* that I'd bor-
row from the library.

DOWN IN THE rec room, my younger brother and I are listening to Jean Knight's "Don't Talk About Jody," a scratchy
B-side, and we're hooting at the funky bass and the syncopated
falsetto before we know *funky* or *New Orleans Sound*, only
that it gets into us and works its way out irresistibly; we dance
and giggle—but I spy him later, leaning on the chain-link fence
between our yard and the Roeloffs', staring into the middle
distance, his self-consciousness promising that more misery
awaits. You see, I'm in the back screen porch now, I'd come
out to get a cookie, or to let Molly in, and I see him alone at the
fence. He's a half-familiar figure in the middle distance. Had he
just come back from his psychiatrist? Had he obsessed again,
erasing and erasing and erasing his crossed-out homework list
until it shredded? *I promised myself I wouldn't do that again.*
What was he thinking at the fence, at the border between?

FAMILY LORE IS that my younger brother took his first steps
as a toddler when he let go of the stereo console in the living room. He'd been peering in at the record going round and

round, turned, and, grinning, wobbled a few steps and fell. His defining moment. His origin story. Mine is this: my younger brother took his first steps as a toddler when he let go of the stereo console in the living room. He'd been peering in at the record going round and round, turned, and, grinning, wobbled a few steps and fell, and I wonder whether this is true, if whether stories we tell about the family matter because they happened or because they have the richness of fiction, its possibilities and playfulness and contrivances, its funny endings and thoughtful themes, because they take root and grow, propagating in all manner of random urgencies, story-seeds flying and landing and nourishing in surprising places to grow even stronger and brighter next year. Beauty no less valuable, no less useless. My brother's forever turning, forever grinning, forever tumbling—whether it happened that way or not, he's stilled in that version of events. He's told. A story lingers because it matters, whether it occurred as the calendar does or inside an imagined truth that speaks no less accurately.

A BOY IS walking home—from school, from the mall, from his friend's house. It doesn't matter from where. Let's follow him via Google Maps. Use Street View. There he is, his head bent down a bit, his fists lightly tapping a beat against his thighs. He's dreaming of girls, bike rides, heroics, a new past, a different future, another house, cousins he undresses, friends he swears at, bullies he pushes over, nuns he warms to, priests he fears, parties he attends, parks he kisses girls in, being taller, being different, dirty books, being true. . . . Right now the sun in sweeping rays renders him invisible. When he arrives home, he walks through the front door and into the kitchen outwardly unchanged. The lives that became truths, the wishes dramatized, the reality only in his head—how is that not also his truth? And what of the man who remembers him now?

THAT NIGHT AFTER homework, and maybe a little *Monday Night Football*, he's in bed and the buses rush past outside and the cold of late fall sneaks in through the window and into his head, wrapping his daydreams in a kind of protective gauze, and there is a feeling, a sensibility, an intuition, a foreign language—murmuring, really, in something that feels like language but may be fever or another dream or a fantasy, an outlined grown-up with a familiar face but a silent mouth moving, talking at him, a kind of knowledge just beyond his fingers—as soon as the glimmer arrives it goes, and he's back to the music of waking life.

NOTES

FIELD RECORDINGS FROM THE INSIDE

"Certainly recorded music haunts us almost by definition. . . ."
Michelle Banks, "Animals in Time: Neko Case and the Contemporary
Country," *PopMatters*, May 11, 2008.

Kathryn Harrison, "The Forest of Memory," *Salmagundi*, no. 152,
Fall 2006.

James Baldwin, "Sonny's Blues," *Going to Meet the Man* (Dial, 1965).

JOURNEY TO THE MOON

Journey to the Moon (Buddah, 1969).

Gerard Degroot, *Dark Side of the Moon: The Magnificent Madness of
the American Lunar Quest* (New York University Press, 2006).

Ian Dove, "Buddah Names in Tie-In Deals," *Billboard*, Novemeber 6,
1971.

IN THE MORNING I'LL RISE ABOVE

Ishmon Bracey's first name is often incorrectly spelled "Ishman."
Bracey's wife Annie corrected the record in an interview with blues
historian Gayle Dean Wardlow in Wardlow's book *Chasin' That Devil
Music*. According to Annie Bracey, her husband was named after a figure in the Old Testament.

The "overheard" song lyrics are from, respectively, "Down Home Girl" (Jerry Leiber and Artie Butler) and "I'm Going to Live the Life I Sing About in My Song" (Thomas A. Dorsey); I'm quoting from Greg Cartwright's blazing solo version, after Mahalia Jackson's.

Gayle Dean Wardlow, *Chasin' That Devil Music: Searching for the Blues* (Backbeat, 1998).

Robert Santelli, *The Big Book of Blues: A Biographical Encyclopedia* (Penguin, 1994).

Paul Kingsbury, ed., *The Encyclopedia of Country Music* (Oxford University Press, 2012).

Bill Malone, *Country Music U.S.A.* (University of Texas Press, 2010).

Adam Komorowski, liner notes, *Groovie Boogie Woogie Boy: Webb Pierce* (Proper Introduction, 2004).

Colin Escott, liner notes, *Country and Western Hit Parade: Dim Lights, Thick Smoke and Hillbilly Music, 1950* (Bear Family, 2008).

Jim Keltner's comments can be heard at "Jerry Lee Lewis: Rock Legend Keeps Rolling," NPR's *Weekend Edition*, September 25, 2010.

Information on the Nighthawks can be found online at *1960s Garage Bands* and *AHS '58 Sandies*.

BAFFLEMENT, CLARITY, AND MALICE

Timothy White, "Elvis Costello: A Man Out of Time Beats the Clock," *Musician* (October 1983).

Elvis Costello, liner notes, "A picture of decay . . ." *Girls+£÷Girls=$&Girls* (Demon, 1989).

"It was being an 'adult' that was most of the problem. . . ." Elvis Costello, liner notes, *Imperial Bedroom* (Rhino, 2002).

Rob Bowman, *Soulsville U.S.A.: The Story of Stax Records* (Schirmer Books, 1987).

Robert Gordon, *Respect Yourself: Stax Records and the Soul Explosion* (Bloomsbury, 2013).

Sam Moore and Dave Marsh, *Sam and Dave: An Oral History* (Avon Books, 1998).

Laura Emerick, "Elvis, Big Stars Create Another 'Spectacle,'" *Chicago Sun-Times*, December 6, 2009.

Peter Handke, *The Jukebox & Other Essays on Storytelling* (Farrar, Straus and Giroux, 1994).

Ellis Nassour, *Honky Tonk Angel: The Intimate Story of Patsy Cline* (Chicago Review Press, 2008).

Costello's version of "She's Got You" (as "He's Got You") appears on the mammoth bonus disc of *Almost Blue* (Rhino, 2004).

LAMB AND LESTER

Charles Lamb, "New Year's Eve," *Essays of Elia* (University of Iowa Press, 2003).

Lester Bangs, "New Year's Eve," *Psychotic Reactions and Carburetor Dung*, edited by Greil Marcus (Vintage, 1988).

HOW TO BE POWERFUL AND TRIUMPHANT AND LONELY ALL AT THE SAME TIME: THE MANY CHANGES OF GREG CARTWRIGHT

Unless noted, all quotations are from conversations with JB.

Information about the naming of Elvis Presley Boulevard from the *Times-News* (Hendersonville, North Carolina), June 9, 1971.

Information about the history of Frayser, Tennessee, from *Frayser: A Turning Point*, Comprehensive Planning Studio, Fall 2006, Graduate Program in City and Regional Planning, University of Memphis.

"Seriously, if it weren't for my wife . . ." Jordan Reyes, *Delayed Gratification* (2012).

"When I was just six years old . . ." Rich Tupica, *Turn It Down*, 2009.

"When I was a kid listening to oldies radio . . ." David Bevan, *Scion 3*, 2011.

For a solid overview of Compulsive Gamblers' and the Oblivians' histories and their place in the garage punk underground, see Eric Davidson's terrific *We Never Learn: The Gunk Punk Undergut, 1988–2001* (Backbeat, 2010).

Stanley Booth, *Rythm Oil: A Journey Through the Music of the American South* (Vintage, 1993).

Information about Danny Burk and the Invaders' "Ain't Going Nowhere" from Ron Hall, *Playing for a Piece of the Door: A History of Garage & Frat Bands in Memphis, 1960–1975* (Shangri-La, 2011).

Greil Marcus, *The History of Rock 'n' Roll in Ten Songs* (Yale University Press, 2014).

". . . not convincingly. Everything I write about . . ." Tupica.

"When you make a big mistake, it never leaves your mind completely. . . ." Austin L. Ray, *Creative Loafing*, 2013.

"I can write a handful of party songs . . ." John Jurgensen, *Wall Street Journal*, June 26, 2014.

"It had water damage . . ." Joe Boone, "The Easley-McCain Era: Two Memphis Engineers Influence the World," *Memphis Flyer*, June 5, 2014.

"The albums, they were really strange. . . ." Tupica.

"That keeps things right where I like it . . ." Fred Mills, *Detroit Metro Times*, 2004.

"All these people asked me . . ." Ryan Leach, *Bored Out*, 2014.

BRAND NEW CADILLAC

"Brand New Cadillac" (Vince Taylor), the Clash, *London Calling* (CBS/Epic, 1979).

HUNTING LARRY HUNTING HANK

Unless noted below, all quotations are from conversations with JB.

"I love a great song, man. Oh yeah. . . ." "Barry Hannah, Brad Watson, and Larry Brown: The Radio Session," in *Conversations with Larry Brown*, edited by Jay Watson (University Press of Mississippi, 2007).

"I've always been a big fan. . . ." "Q&A/Larry Brown: Mounting Tension Is Critical to Storytelling," *Atlanta Journal-Constitution*, September 28, 2003.

"We have relied on Hank Williams . . ." review of Don Cusic, *Hank Williams: The Complete Lyrics*, *Journal of Country Music* 16 (1993). Reprinted in *The Hank Williams Reader*, edited by Patrick Huber, Steve Goodson, and David M. Anderson (Oxford University Press, 2014).

". . . their ability to transport you to other times and other places . . ." lecture given at the Lafayette County–Oxford Library, April 13, 1997, unpublished. Courtesy of Lafayette County–Oxford Library.

". . . a mixtape of sorts . . ." Bloodshot Records press release, "Bloodshot Records to Release *Just One More: A Musical Tribute to Larry Brown*, 19 Songs Celebrating a Great American Writer on May 22, 2007—Artists Include Alejandro Escovedo, Robert Earl

Keen, T-Model Ford, Vic Chesnutt, North Mississippi Allstars & Greg Brown," January 29, 2007.

"Larry absolutely loved music. . . ." Bloodshot Records press release.

"You ask what makes our kind of music successful. . . ." Rufus Jarman, "Country Music Goes to Town," *Nation's Business*, February 1953.

"What they asked me to do . . . That's what I come up with." Marc Fitten and Lawrence Hetrick, conducted for *Chattahoochee Review*, unpublished, in *Conversations with Larry Brown*.

Losing the screenplay to a corrupt file, Larry Brown in a letter to Clyde Edgerton, dated March 10, 2003. Courtesy of Clyde Edgerton.

"I'm doing pretty good, I reckon. . . ." "Q&A/Larry Brown: Mounting Tension Is Critical to Storytelling."

Colin Escott, with George Merritt and William MacEwen, *Hank Williams: The Biography* (Little Brown, 1994).

MAMA LOVED THE WAYS OF THE WORLD

Unless noted, all quotations are from conversations with JB.

Bennie Hess's biography was derived from "Bennie Hess" by Klaus Kettner with Tony Wilkinson and can be found online at *BlackCat Rockabilly Europe*.

Lyrics to "Go-Go Boots" courtesy of Patterson Hood. All attempts were made to obtain copyright permission for the full lyrics to "Please Don't Go Topless, Mother."

LEARNING EMPATHY WITH SINATRA

Sinatra's Swingin' Session!!! (Capitol, 1961).

Francis Albert Sinatra & Antonio Carlos Jobim (Reprise, 1967).

"It Happens Every Spring," B-side (Columbia, 1949).

ACKNOWLEDGMENTS

THANKS TO DAN Smetanka, Deborah Kenmore, Bethany Onsgard, Joe Goodale, Kelly Winton, Barrett Briske, and everyone at Counterpoint/Soft Skull Press, to Matt Roberts, Sophie Beck, and Petra Meyer-Frazier at *The Normal School*, and, especially, to Steven Church, without whom it's likely this book wouldn't exist. Above all, thanks to Amy, for everything.

Thanks also to the many folk who answered questions, engaged me in conversations, or otherwise helped these essays come into being, including Rich Tupica, John Bresland, Paul Bonomo, Michael Montalto, Marty Rogers, Steve Fisher, Greg Fisher, Buck Parr, Shane Brown, Mary Annie Brown-Foshee, Jay Watson, Jean W. Cash, Tom Rankin, and the guys and gals at the Loyal Order of Rock 'n' Roll Freaks (Cheers, Ted Cogswell). Thanks also to the librarians at the Lafayette County–Oxford Public Library, the Archives and Special Collections at the J.D. Williams Library at the University of Mississippi in Oxford, Mississippi, and Founders Library at Northern Illinois University in DeKalb, Illinois.

I'm grateful to the editors at the following journals where these essays first appeared, some in different form: *The Normal School* ("Field Recordings from the Inside," "Sonic Boy" [under the title "In Which I'm Skeptical of Edward Hopper, Who Said, 'The Only Real Influence I've Ever Had Was Myself'"], "Hold Your Phone to This Essay and Select Tag Now," "Don't You Know That It's So?" "In the Morning I'll Rise Above," "Bafflement, Clarity, and Malice," "How to Be Powerful and Triumphant and Lonely All at the Same Time: The Many Changes of Greg Cartwright," "Hunting Larry Hunting Hank," and "Mama Loved the Ways of the World"), *The Rumpus* ("Journey to the Moon"), and *The Essay Review* ("Lamb and Lester"). The "Beatles Girl" section in "Fantasy Park" is text of a video-essay that originally appeared online at *TriQuarterly*.

Some of the "Origin Stories" first appeared in *Creative Nonfiction*, *Hotel Amerika*, *Pithead Chapel*, and *The Rumpus* and on *No Such Thing As Was*, in some cases in different versions.

"I Would Have Had to Have Been a Different Person to Listen to Hüsker Dü," "Learning Empathy with Sinatra," and the first and last segments of "Fantasy Park" originally appeared on *No Such Thing As Was*, in some cases in different versions.

"Brand New Cadillac" appeared in *Clash by Night: A London Calling Anthology*, edited by Gerry LaFemina and Gregg Wilhelm.